TRUE
IN SIX GI

HANNAH'S Girls

Ann
(1833-1897)

Ruth Vitrano Merkel

REVIEW AND HERALD® PUBLISHING ASSOCIATION
HAGERSTOWN, MD 21740

Copyright © 2006 by
Review and Herald® Publishing Association
All rights reserved

The Review and Herald Publishing Association publishes biblically-based materials for spiritual, physical, and mental growth and Christian discipleship.

The author assumes full responsibility for the accuracy of all facts and quotations as cited in this book.

This book was
Edited by Penny Estes Wheeler
Designed by Tina M. Ivany
Cover illustration by Matthew Archambault
Electronic makeup by Shirley M. Bolivar
Typeset: Goudy 13/16

PRINTED IN U.S.A.
10 09 08 07 06   5 4 3 2 1

R&H Cataloging Service
Merkel, Ruth Vitrano
    Ann

   1. Seventh-day Adventists—Biography.   2. Seventh-day Adventists—History.   I. Title   II. Series: Hannah's Girls

286.73209

ISBN 10: 0-8280-1951-7
ISBN 13: 978-0-8280-1951-4

Dedication

To my daughters,
Elaine and Marcia,
&
To my grandchildren,
Erin, Benjamin, and Bradley

To order additional copies of *Hannah's Girls: Ann* (Book 1), by Ruth Merkel, call 1-800-765-6955.

Visit us at www.reviewandherald.com for information on other Review and Herald® products.

Contents

Chapter 1: The Night the Stars Fell / 11

Chapter 2: Mother Tells a Secret / 18

Chapter 3: How Grandpa Got a Dog / 24

Chapter 4: Goodbye, Grandpa / 32

Chapter 5: Ann Makes a Friend / 37

Chapter 6: Wagons, Ho / 44

Chapter 7: First Day on the Trail / 48

Chapter 8: Walking, Walking / 52

Chapter 9: Making Music / 58

Chapter 10: Trouble / 64

Chapter 11: Toby Gets Hurt / 67

Chapter 12: Independence Day / 81

Chapter 13: Mrs. Weston to the Rescue / 86

Chapter 14: Rascal / 90

Chapter 15: Almost Home / 98

Chapter 16: The End of the Trail / 101

The Rest of Ann's Story / 106

More About Ann's World / 109

Introduction

My 16-year-old granddaughter, Erin, is a sixth generation Seventh-day Adventist girl, a descendent of Ann of this book. *Ann* is the first in a series of six books. Each book tells the story of a girl in these six generations. Through their stories you will see God's abundant providence and His protection and love for His children.

The first story is about my great-grandmother, Ann, who saw the stars fall in 1833. The last book is about my granddaughter, Erin, who saw Hale Bopp Comet.

—*Ruth Merkel*

Hannah's Girls Family Tree

Hannah = Willard Eddy
(1816-1897)

Ann = John Turner
(1838-1897)

— Marilla = Henry Parfitt
(1851-1916)
— Oscar
— Osra

Ida, Annie, James, Daisy, Pearl, Bessie, Nettie, Edwin, John, Grace = Justus Vitrano
(1890-1973)

Genevieve, Steven, Ruth = Eugene Merkel
(1981-)

Elaine = Dann Hotelling — Marcia
(1961-)

Erin, Benjamin, Bradley
(1988-)

Annie Laurie

Generation One

Ann
(1833-1897)

ERIN'S GREAT-GREAT-GREAT-GRANDMOTHER

Some of the people you'll meet in Ann...

- **ANN EDDY:** pioneer girl
- **OSCAR AND OZRO:** Ann's younger brothers
- **WILLARD EDDY:** Ann's father, a blacksmith
- **HANNAH EDDY:** Ann's mother
- **GRANDPA EDDY:** grandpa to Ann, Oscar, and Ozro
- **MR. HATHAWAY:** the wagon master
- **HAWKEYE:** wagon train scout, rides at the front of the wagon train
- **LUTHER ST. JOHN (LUTE):** wagon scout, rides at the rear of the wagon train
- **JULIE DUNBAR:** the answer to Ann's prayer
- **DOC WILLOUGHBY:** traveled with the wagon train
- **THE WESTONS:** a rowdy, unkempt family with two sons, Toby and Edgar

ONE

The Night the Stars Fell

Once upon a time, a long time ago, in a small house in southern New York State, there lived a baby girl named Ann Eddy.

One chilly November night Ann's mother, Hannah, gently rocked her in the big chair near the hearth where a cheery fire warmed the room with a cozy glow. Ann's little eyelids grew heavy with sleep as she snuggled against her mother's shoulder and listened to the sweet lullaby:

> "Sleep, my child, and peace attend thee,
> All through the night;
> Guardian angels God will send thee,
> All through the night . . . ."

On the warm hearth, curled up—her paws tucked neatly under her small body—sat the calico cat. Her eyes were narrowed in sleep, and her fluffy tail wrapped securely around her body.

Father Willard read his Bible by the light from the crackling fire. All was tranquil and calm. Mother quietly placed Ann in her little bed. She serenely slept on this, one of the most important nights of her life.

Ann: 1833-1897

Some time during the wee hours of the morning, the dogs began to bark. "They must have a raccoon up a tree," Father sleepily muttered as he rolled over in bed. But in the distance he heard neighbor dogs join in the barking. Sleepily, he decided to get up and see what was going on.

Opening his eyes, he saw light streaming through the window. In fact, the room was so light that he saw their clock ticking on the shelf. It was after midnight. It certainly was not time to get up.

But why was it so bright outside? He slipped out of bed and went to the window. To his amazement the sky was filled with thousands of falling stars.

"Wake up, Hannah," he whispered excitedly. "Come look at the sky. Something unbelievable is happening."

Hannah was astonished. Stars were falling everywhere. The sky looked like a giant umbrella of shooting stars.

Quickly putting on their coats, they stepped out into the yard. Outside, they heard distant thunder and crackling sounds as the biggest stars streaked toward the horizon. Hannah clutched her husband's arm. They were speechless and bewildered.

"Willard! Hannah!" came the shouts of neighbor men hurrying down the road. "We were hoping you'd be up. The parson is opening the church so we can meet there to pray. He thinks this is a sign that the Lord is coming!" The men rushed down the road to spread the word to others.

Hannah's eyes widened. If the Lord was truly on His way to earth, she didn't want little Ann to miss seeing the glorious event. Snugly wrapping baby Ann in a warm blanket, Mother took her outdoors. Father pointed to the sky, and Ann's sleepy eyes brightened with excitement. She clapped her small hands and smiled with delight.

It was November 13, 1833.

No, Jesus did not come that night. But for a long time everyone who'd seen it talked of nothing else but the shower of stars.

Willard and Hannah faithfully continued to study their Bible. They felt encouraged by the words of Jesus found in Matthew 24:29. This text is Jesus' answer to the question His disciples asked about the signs of His second coming. Jesus said that one of the signs would be stars falling from heaven. Willard and Hannah treasured this text for the rest of their lives, and repeated it to their children.

When Ann was about 9 years old, her father listened with great interest to a man who'd traveled to the untamed Northwest Territory. He said that the soil was so rich that seeds sprouted almost overnight. There were so many deer and wild turkeys that they practically begged to be eaten. All these good things were just waiting, he said, for people bold enough to face the danger of living in an untamed land.

While some were doubtful, Willard was not daunted. Yes, pioneers to a new land would live without modern conveniences. But Willard, a tall, muscular, gentle man, was as strong as they came. He was a blacksmith, and used to hard work. In fact, for generations, all the men in his family had been blacksmiths. He'd grown up smelling the pungent smoke of his father's shop and hearing the mur-

Ann: 1833-1897

mur and trickle of water as it poured over his uncle's slow-turning stone grist mill next to the forge.

Although she was small, Ann's mother, Hannah, was hardy and hard-working. She agreed with her husband that they could be successful in the new land. Instead of being fearful, they were excited by the possibilities. Three other neighbor families decided to travel west as well— the Sacketts, the Grants, and the Russells. They all would go with Mr. Page Hathaway, a wagon master from Albany who was leading a group heading to the mid-West in the late spring.

After church one sunny autumn day the family sat on their front porch talking about their up-coming journey while enjoying the unexpected lovely warm afternoon. They knew that Indian summer would end, but for now they soaked up the sun. The sugar maples and oaks were brilliant with bright red and orange leaves. The leaves of the poplar trees fluttered and whispered in the breeze. Robins hopped along the ground, cocking their heads as they listened for worms. Blue jays called noisily while flitting from tree to tree.

Mother and Father slowly creaked back and forth in their wooden swing. The children sprawled on the floor with the family dog, Dixie, who lay with his head resting on Ann's knee. His sleepy eyes opened now and again just to gaze happily at the family members.

As the young parents quietly looked over their children, Willard picked up Ann's hand and held it in his. As they'd considered pulling up stakes and leaving everything they knew, they'd prayed fervently that the Lord would help them know whether to stay or to go. They wanted to do what was best for their children.

Ann was a year older than Oscar, but they could have passed as twins with their light brown hair, sparkling blue eyes, and the freckles sprinkled across their noses. Mother often said that the two children were like peas in a pod. They frequently heard her laughingly exclaim, "I declare, you are both just full of mischief and shenanigans! What one of you doesn't think of to do, t'other one does."

Ann and Oscar laughed to hear her say it. Her smile always told them that she wasn't upset.

Their little brother Ozro had darker hair but the same blue eyes. Whatever Oscar did, Ozro tried to do, too. Whatever Oscar said, Ozro always agreed to. Ann and Oscar usually let him tag along on their quests for adventure, though sometimes it took a lot of coaxing from their parents to convince them to do so.

Ann broke the spell of the pleasant, quiet afternoon. "I'm so glad Nellie and Erv Sackett and Herb and little Nancy are going west with us," she told her family. "I think Nellie's pretty, and Erv is always happy, whistling a merry tune. Little Nancy's walking already. She's cute."

"This morning Erv told me that Nellie's brother Pete has decided to join them," Father told her.

"Hooray," shouted Oscar. "I'll have someone to turn cartwheels with!"

Pete Edminster was a lively young man who loved to tumble. He had taught Oscar to stand on his head, walk

Ann: 1833-1897

on his hands, and how to do flips. Oscar learned quickly, and Pete said he was a natural-born acrobat.

Since Nellie and Erv were their nearest neighbors, the two families knew each other well. Pete was often at his sister's home and at the Eddy's, also.

"That Pete is going to be a splendid catch for some young woman whenever he decides to settle down," Mother said. "But I'm glad he is taking his time. He'll find someone—or she'll find him," she laughed. "Pete can be comical and playful, but he's energetic and dependable too."

Ann turned thoughtful. "If only Thelma and Agnes weren't so young," she sighed. "I'm praying that there'll be a girl my age in the wagon train. Don't you suppose there will be?"

"Well, I reckon there just might be," answered her father. "But don't worry. Time will tell." He gave her a fond smile. "Those little Grant girls look up to you, Ann. They think you're half-way grown, Honey Girl." Ann loved the little nickname her father had given her. It made her feel special.

"By the way, Hannah, when last I spoke with Pa, he suggested we might leave Dixie with him," Father said.

Ann was stunned speechless. Dixie had been with the family since he was just a pup. Part Spitz, all black with a plumy tail that wagged almost constantly, he was both gentle with the children and an excellent watch dog.

Ann's fingers pushed deeply into the thick fur on Dixie's neck. She felt like her heart would stop. She couldn't breathe. Feeling the sudden tug of Ann's fingers,

The Night the Stars Fell

Dixie looked up at her while his tail thumped and brushed the porch floor. He was her dog. His heart belonged to her, and her's to him. It had always been that way.

Never, never, she thought, shuddering at the idea of parting with him.

Mother's reaction was immediate and strong.

"Why the very idea, Will!" she protested. "Dixie's part of our family, and we'll not be leaving him behind," she said firmly. "That's that." As usual, she was very decided in her opinions.

All the children were listening closely, their eyes wide with concern. When Father replied with an easy smile, "Well then, I see it's settled. Dixie will come with us," they jumped off the porch and ran circles to celebrate.

"Hooray, hooray, hooray for Dixie!" they cheered, waving their arms with relief. Oscar turned cartwheels and Ozro tried doing somersaults. Dixie sensed their excitement and ran with them, jumping and barking. When the children fell down exhausted, he licked their faces.

Ann looked up at the sky and fervently whispered, "Thank You, God in heaven. Thank You."

TWO

Mother Tells a Secret

So began the long days of sorting, packing, and planning. Autumn slipped by and now it was winter. Eager for spring, the short, cold days seemed to drag by for the little family, but they used their time wisely.

Father started making a list. "Hannah, I think we should take a small tent to sleep in. It will keep us dry at night when it rains," he told her. "Of course, on warm nights the children and I can sleep out under the wagon."

"And," added Mother, "wouldn't it be good to take a couple of small, folding canvas stools to sit on so we don't always have to squat on the ground?"

They arranged to sell their house and the chickens to Uncle Barack and Aunt Rebecca, Father's younger brother and his wife. Barack would now take over the the family blacksmith shop.

"What will we do without you here in the shop, Will?" Barack had asked. "You know all the tricks of the trade."

Father laughed. "You will do just fine. You've worked next to me all your life. Now it's your turn to be the village smithy. Pa will advise, so never fear. He still loves to be involved, and the neighbors like to have him in the

Mother Tells a Secret

shop occasionally." Will closed his eyes and saw his dad near the bellows, leaning forward on a stool. "His words of wit and wisdom are welcomed by everyone," he added, and Barack agreed.

Father bought a wagon—a prairie schooner, it was called. Attached to the rectangular wagon were tall hoops to hold up the canvas cover. The ends of the cover would be open by day and in good weather. At either end of the canvas were stout strings that could be drawn tight for privacy or to keep out wind and rain.

Ann immediately climbed into the wagon to see what it looked like inside. "How will we fit everything in?" she asked. "It's big, but not nearly as big as our house."

"We'll have to leave some things behind, Ann. That's going to be the hard part," her mother said, thinking of furniture and other precious things that they wouldn't have room to take.

"Why are the front wheels smaller than the rear wheels?" Oscar wondered. Father explained that was so the wagon could easily make sharp turns.

The wonderful wagon was kept in the barn all winter so it would be out of the stormy weather. Oscar helped Father build cupboards that just fit along the sides inside the wagon. They'd hold things the family needed such as their pots and pans, a skillet, and a Dutch oven with a lid—used for cooking, and baking leftovers for stews.

Even young Ozro kept busy by running errands back and forth.

While Father was occupied with things he had to do to

Ann: 1833-1897

get ready for the trip, in her spare time Mother was sewing. With needle and thread in hand and fabric lying across her lap, she worked by the light of the winter sun slanting through the living room windows. For Will and the boys, she made shirts and pants. For herself and Ann, she made calico dresses and gingham dresses. Then she made pinafores to wear over them, to keep the dresses clean. Though the room was sometimes chilly, her thoughts ran forward to the sunny days they'd spend walking next to their wagon on the way to the Northwest Territory.

"Ann, I'm making sunbonnets to help keep the sun out of our eyes," she told her daughter. It was a little tricky working with the stiff brims of the bonnets, but she managed. "If the strings bother you, just let them hang loose."

"Thanks, Mama," Ann said, glancing at the bright bonnets. "They really are pretty. I'll wear them." She sighed. "It's just that bonnets make me feel so hedged in. I'd just as soon plop a straw hat on my head like the boys do."

She gently stroked the dresses Mother had carefully placed on the bed. "All my new dresses are nice but you know, I think I like this blue and white one the best." Ann held it against her and looked in the wall mirror. "It reminds me of the color of the sky. My blue socks will match."

Mother smiled at her blue-eyed daughter and thought, *The dress will match your eyes too.*

Ann had learned to knit and crochet when she was quite young. Grandma Eddy had seen to that. Ann was Grandma's namesake, and there had always been a special

Mother Tells a Secret

bond between them. Ann liked knitting better than crocheting, and knitted socks for each member of the family so they'd be well stocked for their up-coming trip.

Out of the goodness of her heart she'd also knit a pair of socks each for Thelma and Agnes Grant. She'd given them to the girls for Christmas.

"Oh, how beautiful they are. They're just perfect. They're the most wonderful socks in the world," Thelma had exclaimed, clutching the socks to her chest. She greatly admired Ann and in her girlish way tried to imitate her, much to Ann's dismay. "Imitation is Thelma's way of paying you a compliment," Mother had explained, but Ann didn't always find that a comfort.

"I know Thelma means well, Mama, but sometimes I want to tell her to go away and leave me alone. She's worse than a little fruit fly darting around my head that I can't get rid of."

Oscar had howled in laughter at that.

But out of the kindness of her young heart, Ann tried to cheerfully endure Thelma's good intentions.

"It's best to suffer in silence than to hurt Thelma's feelings," Mother had advised. And when Oscar ran off to play with Ozro, Mother had Ann sit down so they could talk.

"I'm going to tell you something, Ann, and 'tis best if we keep this between us. You are getting old enough to understand family matters."

Ann bit her lower lip, wondering what her mother was going to say.

"Your grandma had a real time tryin' to be patient with

Mrs. Abernathy," Mother began gently. "When Mrs. Abernathy got on her high horse about some issue—whether in church or out of church—your grandma would get a certain look to her face. She'd set her jaw rigidlike and never utter a word—until we got home. Then she'd rave a bit, and Grandpa would chuckle about it. He always was more tolerant and forbearing with people."

"Really, Mama?" Ann was interested. "I kind of remember those two ladies jawing at each other one time about putting the church bell in the steeple. Mrs. Abernathy just walked off, huffylike, and Grandma pushed her hat down tight on her head and took Grandpa's hand and climbed into the wagon." Ann smiled, remembering the event, and Mother laughed.

"Oh, there was a real to-do about that. But I recall today just as though it was yesterday what your grandma said. 'Tis better for a soul to suffer in silence and be possessed in patience rather than have to eat your words,' is what she told me. She truly tried to live by the Golden Rule—you know, Do unto others as you would have them do unto you." Mama looked wistful and Ann knew she was feeling sad that Grandma was no longer with them. "She treated me like I was one of her daughters, and I loved her for that. But she struggled with her tongue, Ann, and in all honesty I must say she usually won."

Mother shook her head. "But oh how she could use a well-chosen, pointed word when it was necessary!" she added with a grin.

"Grandma was so sweet to me. I never thought of her

Mother Tells a Secret

as having to overcome anything," Ann said, remembering the grandmother who'd died hardly a year before.

"You were her own flesh and blood, Ann. Her first-born grandchild. You held a very dear place in her heart. So pay heed to Grandma's words and try to understand Thelma." Mother leaned over and patted Ann's hand. "You aren't obliged to linger around every time she comes, though. After a bit, just excuse yourself and leave the room. That's called charity and self-control."

"The patience of Job's a real thing, isn't it, Mama?"

They laughed together, and Mother hugged her young daughter. "Mercy, child! You are growing up before my eyes."

Mama also has a way with words herself, thought Ann.

THREE

How Grandpa Got a Dog

Springtime found the Eddy household as busy as a beehive. "Why can't we leave right now?" Oscar asked, anxious to get going now that the weather was warmer.

"Mr. Hathaway knows best, son," Father answered. "We have to wait. There has to be plenty of grass along the trail for the animals to eat. We simply could not take along enough food for them. It's to our advantage to cooperate with nature."

Father oiled the wagon's canvas cover to make it waterproof, and he greased the wheels. He hung a few extra hooks on the wooden hoops so there'd be places to hang their jackets and hats, the milk cans, lanterns, and anything else that they had room to take.

"I understand that it'll be easy to churn butter while we travel," Father said with a chuckle.

"What do you mean, Papa?" Ann was curious.

"Well, we'll hang a pail of cream on a hook at the rear of the wagon. By the end of the day the cream will have turned to butter while the wagon swings, jostles, and jolts its way along. Doesn't that sound easy?"

Oscar looked at his father from the corner of his eyes.

How Grandpa Got a Dog

"You don't mean it," he said, doubtful. "Are you joshin' us, Papa?"

"Are you joshin' us?" repeated young Ozro

"I'm dead serious. Apparently it really works. We'll have to try it and prove it ourselves once we're on the road."

Ted Grant, Thelma's and Agnes' father, was both a family friend and a cooper. He made or repaired barrels. So Father bought from him an extra barrel for the trip, some pails, and a washtub. Mother filled the new barrel with sawdust and packed their breakable things in it.

Ann helped her mother pack the barrels with the meat they'd dried, salted, or smoked. They also packed flour, cornmeal, beans, sugar, salt, and dried apples, peaches, and pears.

"Potatoes and eggs will last for a while," said Mother, "but eggs won't travel well. Perhaps we should pack them in the flour barrel at the last minute."

"Can we take enough food with us to last the whole trip?" Oscar liked eating!

"We can pick berries, nuts, and wild onions along the way," Father told him, "but you have to be very careful about what berries you pick so you don't eat poisonous ones. I've shown you the eatable ones. A good rule to follow is, when in doubt, don't."

Young Ozro piped up. "Pete told me t'other day I could catch fish with him. I'll catch hundreds for us to eat." Ozro was given to exaggeration. He rubbed circles on his tummy while reciting,

Fishy, fishy in the brook, Papa caught him with a hook.

Ann: 1833-1897

Mama fries him in a pan, Baby eats 'em like a man."

Mother smiled. "Why you little whippersnapper! Hundreds of fish you say? Remember, my young man, not to count your chickens before they hatch."

※

On sunny days, Ann enjoyed sitting in the wagon daydreaming about their upcoming trip. *It's beginning to look just like a wagon house,* she thought.

Mother explained that she planned to place her table on a braided rug in the middle of the wagon. And right behind and under the seat area she'd put her precious wedding trunk. Ann could visualize just what it all would look like. Sometimes she served imaginary tea from an imaginary silver teapot to the imaginary friend she hoped to meet on the trip west.

One day they all went to Grandpa Eddy's to spend the afternoon. He lived not far away, in a little house next to Uncle Barack and Aunt Rebecca who looked after him now that Grandma was gone.

The children loved going to see their grandfather. In his spare time, he whittled and carved, and was well known among the neighbors for this hobby. All three of the children enjoyed playing with the little wood shavings that curled up and dropped on the floor as he worked. Ann liked to hold them up by her ears and pretend they were long curls.

Grandpa told the best stories, especially the scary tales about his military duties during the Revolutionary War.

How Grandpa Got a Dog

"Please, Grandpa, tell us about your dog, 'Watch,' just one more time," they begged him today. In the back of their minds they felt sad because Grandpa wasn't going west with them. They might never see him again.

So, lifting Ozro upon his knee, and getting that thoughtful, long-ago-far-away look in his eyes, Grandpa once more told the tale they loved best.

"I was just 16 years old when I served in the Rhode Island militia. My assignment was to guard the Newport coast to keep the Tories from landing. I patrolled the shoreline—sometimes by myself at night."

Even though she knew the story by heart, Ann could almost feel the hair rise on the back of her neck as he continued.

"One dark, moonless night I'd been patrolling and had momentarily stopped to rest my back against a huge oak tree. I heard an owl hoot nearby, and a bat swooped across the darkness. Crickets were chirping, and all seemed peaceful-like and serene when suddenly, but surely, I heard a strange rustle in the bushes behind me. I turned with a start. What was it?" His voice grew lower. He was almost whispering. "Barely breathing, I waited and listened. There it was again!"

Ozro could not wait another minute for Grandpa to go on. "Were your knees knocking and your feet shaking in your boots?" he asked.

"Sh-h-h, Ozro," said Ann, "let Grandpa finish the story."

"Yes, siree, sir, I was mighty scared. With my hand on

Ann: 1833-1897

my musket, I shouted, 'Halt! Who goes there?' No reply. Nervously I squinted in the darkness, not seeing a thing. Then suddenly from behind a tree straggled a rangy-looking, yellow dog.

"I laughed in pure relief when I discovered my 'enemy' was a dog. Gently I called, 'Here, fella, come here, you ol' renegade!'"

Even though they'd heard the story many times, the children all sighed with relief. *It was just a dog, not a Tory!*

"At first the dog was wary and only sniffed the air, probably trying to determine if that human being who was talking to him was friend or foe. After a few moments, he slowly approached and rather suspicious-like circled the tree where I stood.

"Now that the dog was up close, I could tell he'd either been in a fight or had been beaten by someone. He limped, and had spots of crusted blood in his fur. He looked awful lean and hungry.

"I took the last crust of bread from my knapsack and offered it to him. 'Here ya' go. Want something to eat. Are ya' hungry?' I asked him.

"I tell ya,' that dog took no time at all to chew and swallow the bread, and then looked at me as if to say, 'Do you have more?'

"I didn't have any more, but I patted him on the head and scratched behind his ears, all the while talking quietly and soothinglike to him. He timidly licked my fingers, then he sat down. By George, that dog was nervous and edgy and jumped at every noise, but he stayed the night."

How Grandpa Got a Dog

Impatient Ozro interrupted with, "And he went home with you, huh, Grandpa?" He already knew the answer, but just wanted to hear it again.

"That's right. And in the morning, when I was relieved of my duty by another guard, the dog followed me. In fact, he never left my side from then on.

"When I went back home to Gloucester, I took the stray dog with me where he became a family pet. We named him, Watch—short for Nightwatch—and he lived to a ripe old age, never going hungry again."

Grandpa sighed with contentment. It was a good story, well told. He'd enjoyed reliving it himself.

"Wish I could'a known ole Watch," Oscar told Grandpa, and Ann nodded her head.

"Ya," agreed Ozro. "I'd of been sure to give him some corn bread if he'd a-been my dog."

"Yes, always be kind to your animals. That's the *eleventh* commandment you know," Grandpa soberly but humorously reminded them.

Grandpa loved animals. The neighbors all knew he would shoe their horses with kindness and care. For many years, his blacksmith shop was a gathering place for tradesmen, friends, and neighbors who came on business or just to sit and talk.

"Remember, children, no man knows a more faithful animal than his horse," Grandpa often told them. Today he reminded them, "Horses never forget kindness, and they always remember injustice and injury. Take good care of your Dolly and Daisy. They're good horses."

Ann: 1833-1897

They nodded obediently.

Then Grandpa took Oscar's hand. "I've noticed how you have worked in the shop helping your pa, and the interest you have shown in shoeing the horses," he told the boy. "You're a good worker, and your love for horses and other animals warms my heart. I'd like nothing more than to have you follow in my footsteps and become a blacksmith just as your father and your Uncle Barack have done."

Oscar smiled proudly.

Still holding Oscar's hand, Grandpa grasped Ozro's hand as well. "While I would be happy to have both of you become blacksmiths, I must say this. Listen well, boys. I'm more interested in having you become honest workmen. Our family is not known for greatness, but it is known for goodness. Remember that. You will both be successful in this life and in the life to come if you are kind to animals, courteous to grownups, considerate of children, and treat the girls and womenfolk with respect. Will you promise me that?"

Both boys answered seriously, "Yes, Grandpa."

"Now then, as for you, Annie, I share the same advice." Holding her head between his gnarled hands, his eyes smiling down a blessing, he told her, "Always be honest, kind, courteous, and respectful. Stay sweet, my child, and let those who will, be clever."

Ann's smile spoke all the words she could not say.

Then Grandpa went to his cupboard. "Here is something I want you to have, Annie. It belonged to your Grandma." He handed Ann a small, beautifully hand-carved trinket box he'd made from balsam wood long ago for his bride. It had the letter "A" carved on the lid.

"Oh, Grandpa, it is lovely," breathed Ann.

Slowly she lifted the lid. Inside was a little gold chain and a lovely linen handkerchief edged with beautiful dainty, lavender lace. Grandma had hand-stitched the handkerchief and crocheted its lace edging. Ann was overwhelmed by the gift.

"Oh, oh," was all she could whisper. Then she turned and leaned into Grandpa's bear hug. He held her for a good long time.

To Oscar and Ozro he gave small hand-carved, hand-painted birds, and for each boy he had a small bag of marbles.

"Look, Annie, I got a cat's eye, some aggies, and a steely for shootin.' Mebbe I can beat Oscar playin' marbles now!" Ozro was excited.

"That'll be the day." Oscar threw back his head and laughed, but in big-brotherly fashion he fondly linked his arm with Ozro's.

The children said "thank you" over and over again.

FOUR

Goodbye, Grandpa

Then while the grownups talked, the children sat at Grandpa's table and admired their gifts. Their minds were already on their upcoming adventures, but a bit of their hearts remained right there with Grandpa. They half listened to the conversation going on around them.

"Be careful, Willard, as you travel. What route will you be taking?" Grandpa wondered aloud.

"At first we'll be on the old Mohawk Trail, then along the southern shore of long Lake Erie. After that we continue through Indiana territory, on to Chicago, then up into Wisconsin territory. And don't worry about us, Pa. We have good, dependable men with us that can repair wheels, wagons, canvas covers, and harnesses. You know the men from around here that will be traveling with us."

Grandpa agreed. "Yes, they are good people." And he counted off on his fingers as he said their names. "Erv Sackett, Pete Edminster, Ted Grant, and as for Henry Russell—I'm sad to see him leave." The old man shook his head. "Even though Henry was born with a silver spoon in his mouth, he's no slouch. He's hard-

Goodbye, Grandpa

working and sharp as a tack. You'd be hard pressed to find a better man, Will. He's leaving his sawmill to be run by his brother, and he plans to start another in the new territory. I understand he has made some plans and preparations already."

The Russells would be traveling alone. Their children were grown.

"Let's not forget the competent womenfolk going along." Mother joined the conversation. "Nellie Sackett is a clever young woman. 'Course, she has to be, to keep up with Erv. Nothing gets past her.

"Irene Grant is quiet but cheerful, agreeable, and hardworking. Her girls are fine ones, too. Thelma, especially, is a pleasant girl, and Agnes is as cute as a bug in a rug with that red hair of hers, and that smile. Those young'uns each pieced a quilt top last winter.

"Charlotte Russell's the very soul of kindness, a right proper woman, and she just loves our children."

Oscar chimed in from his chair at the table and enthusiastically said, "I hope Mrs. Russell takes along her candy dish. Her peppermint sticks are deee-licious!" He smacked his lips and raised his eyebrows up and down.

They all chuckled just watching him.

"Mrs. Russell hugs me too much," Ozro complained, wrinkling his nose. "And she calls me 'dearie' like I was a girl. But at least she's not grouchy like old Mrs. Abernathy. Mrs. Abernathy frowns at me if I wiggle in church."

"Mrs. Abernathy's a critical soul," Grandpa soberly agreed. "She grieves us all. But I suppose if we carried

Ann: 1833-1897

her burdens we'd feel woeful, too."

Ann and her mother looked at each other, remembering their conversation about Grandma and Mrs. Abernathy.

To Father, Grandpa soberly said, "You understand, of course, not everyone's convinced you're making a sane or wise decision, Willard. The Randalls, Mrs. Abernathy, Beatrice and Blanche Longworth—bless their souls . . ." he paused, chuckling. "Then there's Archie and Dewey Lathrop. Every one of 'em cluck their tongues and wonder why people would be willing to give up a working farm, or a church, or business, family members, and good neighbors for uncleared land."

Father gave Grandpa a crooked smile and slapped his knee with enthusiasm.

"But that uncleared land is really cheap! And on top of that we'll have a stake in the new part of our country. That's why we're goin'."

Ann enjoyed seeing her father get excited about their move. She loved her father, and she was proud he was taking such a bold and courageous step, whether others agreed with him or not.

"Well, Lord only knows how I'll miss you," Grandpa declared. "Be sure to take plenty of food," he added. "I don't want these children to go hungry."

There was a thoughtful silence.

Turning to the children, Grandpa told them, "Always think of me when you repeat the 23rd Psalm. And keep working on memorizing Psalm 91, too. I know it's a long

Goodbye, Grandpa

one, but it's wonderful and comforting. Grandma and I used to say it out loud together just for its beauty."

Grandpa loved to memorize verses and passages from the Bible. He knew many, and he could say long poems, too. He praised his grandchildren whenever they learned a new verse of Scripture.

"I already know most of Psalm 91, Grandpa," Ann told him. "Oscar and I have a race on, seein' who can finish it first. My favorite verse is verse four, 'He shall cover thee with His feathers, and under His wings shalt thou trust.' Doesn't that sound just like my old pet hen, Rhody? Lots of times I've seen her tend her baby chicks, clucking for them to come to her and covering them with her feathers. I just loved her."

Grandpa understood. "Yes, that's just the way our God cares for us if we'll let Him."

Too soon the day was over. Everyone hugged and kissed Grandpa a sad goodbye. They did not know if or when they would see him again.

"Train the children in the way they should go, Willard, and send word back as soon as you can," instructed Grandpa. "I'll be anxious."

Then he gathered them in a circle and prayed, "'May the Lord be between me and thee while we are absent one from the other.'" He said the blessing softly while tears ran down his cheeks.

They all dried their eyes and hugged again. It was time to leave. Morning would come before they knew it. It was time to head home.

Ann: 1833-1897

Tonight's the last night. I can hardly wait for tomorrow, Ann thought. *Oh, how I hope to meet up with a girl who will be my special friend.*

Ann slipped on her nightgown, said her prayers, and climbed into bed.

FIVE

Ann Makes a Friend

Before Ann knew it, the sun's rays were gilding the heavens.

How could I have overslept? I wanted to be up with the sun!

She jumped out of bed, ran to the window, looked up at the sky, and stretched her arms over her head. Today was the day! They were packed and ready. She'd have to hurry into her clothes for she surely didn't want to miss the arrival of Mr. Hathaway with the other travelers.

Oscar fed and watered Dolly and Daisy, and hitched them to the wagon. He had groomed them carefully. They were lovely horses to look at with their brown coats and light manes and tails.

The family cow, Pansy, was tethered to the back of the wagon. She stood silently chewing her cud. Her milk was plentiful and delicious, and Father had agreed that Ozro should feed and take care of her on their journey.

Ozro felt proud that he'd been given a special chore. He loved Pansy dearly, even though he was a bit too young to milk her. He had asked his father to make her a new cow bell in the blacksmith shop, and he'd hung it lovingly around her neck. Now he whispered in her ear,

Ann: 1833-1897

"Annie has Dixie, Oscar has Dolly and Daisy, and now I have you, Pansy. You're mine to care for. No other cow will have such a pretty bell as yours."

※

Very early the neighbors arrived—Erv, Nellie, young Herb, little Nancy, and Pete came first. Then came the Grants and the Russells. Everyone was ready and excited. They all talked at once, checked and double-checked their wagons, and examined their animals one more time.

Thelma and Agnes ran to Ann.

"Oh, Annie, ain't this a most wonderful, marvelous day!" Thelma clutched Ann's hand and hopped up and down for joy. "I'm so glad we'll be traveling together. Say, your new dress is pretty, Ann. Blue looks nice on you, and it matches your eyes."

Ann could not help but smile. After all, Thelma was a sincere and loyal little friend. "Thank you Thelma. You look mighty nice yourself today. Excuse me, please, I must speak to Mama."

That was easier than I thought, Ann thought to herself as she walked away.

Soon Pete shouted, "Here they come!"

Ann counted seven wagons. The last one had a sign painted on it, 'Ohio or bust.' The family in this wagon was going only as far as Ohio. She strained her eyes to make out faces of the people up and down the wagon train.

In the first wagon sat a man wearing a type of military uniform. His hat had some gold braid trim across the

Ann Makes a Friend

front. His face was brown from the sun and a little wrinkled, but it was a kind face. He sat tall and straight. He looked so impressive that Ann and Oscar stared wide-eyed at him.

He must be Mr. Hathaway, Ann thought.

On either side of his wagon rode a man on horseback.

One was a big, tall man with a coonskin hat, and he rode a beautiful chestnut mare with black mane and tail. The man's muscles seemed to ripple and show right through his red shirt. He wore spurs and black canvas pants, and appeared to be bigger than life.

"Goliath," Oscar whispered to Ann.

The sun, wind, and rain had made the man's face almost the color of his horse. He was obviously younger than the man in the wagon, but Ann thought he looked strong enough to fight a bear.

The second man wore buckskins and had a feather stuck in his dark, shoulder-length hair. There was something unusual about him—he looked sober, but he wore a shimmer of a smile on his face.

His big, silver horse was energetic and frisky and looked like it could take off at a full gallop if his owner said, "Giddyup!" The horse snorted, tossed and jerked his head, but the man kept him under control.

"He's a fidgety horse," observed Oscar.

"He's fidgety alright, and he jiggles," added Ozro.

Ann and Oscar couldn't keep from smiling at their little brother's choice of words.

Then Ann and Oscar both spotted "her" at the same time.

Ann: 1833-1897

"It's a girl with a bonnet, Oscar," whispered Ann nudging him with her elbow.

"I know, I know, I'm not blind. There's a boy, too, holding the reins." Never one to be shy, Oscar walked right over to the wagon.

Standing stark still, Ann watched as the girl jumped down.

She looks about my size, she thought.

Oscar was introducing himself. Then he pointed back toward Ann, "And that's my sister," she heard him say.

The boy on the wagon seat appeared a bit older than the girl, and when he took off his straw hat and smiled down at Oscar, Ann couldn't believe the color of his hair. It was so blond it looked almost white.

Walking toward the girl, Ann smiled widely. Before she could say a thing, Ozro ran up, pulled at Ann's skirt, and excitedly announced, "See, Annie, it's the girl you prayed for."

The girl's eyebrows went up in surprise, and Ann found herself looking into a pair of the greenest eyes she had ever seen.

The girl smiled, and Ann quickly explained, "It's true. I was so hoping there would be another girl around my age in the wagon train. I'm mighty relieved and grateful to see you. I'm Ann—Ann Eddy—and I'm 10. That was my brother Oscar who came to meet you. This is my little brother."

"I'm happy to meet you, too," the girl answered. "My name's Julia, but most everyone calls me Julie. And that's

Ann Makes a Friend

my brother Chuckie back on the wagon. Our folks are Helen and Dawson Dunbar." As she shoved her bonnet back, Ann discovered that she had hair as light and bright as her brother's.

Leaning over, Julie spoke to Ozro, "And what's your name?" she playfully asked. Ozro shyly ducked his head but spoke right up. "I'm Ozro, and I'm goin' on 5."

Julie smiled and replied, "Well, I'm 10 goin' on 11, and Chuckie's 12 goin' on 13. Our older sister, Orva, didn't come with us. She just got married. Maybe she and Frank will join us next year."

She is my age! Ann could scarcely believe her ears.

Julie continued. "Doc Willoughby is traveling alone in a wagon right behind ours. His wife died a couple years ago. Chuckie drives his wagon for him once in a while to give Doc a rest. He's almost like a member of our family, so he decided to move west with us. He says that folks on the frontier will need a doctor as much as folks do in town."

"I'm excited about this trip. Are you?" Ann asked.

"Well, I guess so," Julie replied. "We lived in town, so I don't know all about country living, but I 'spect I'll have to learn."

The girls walked around, talking like they were old friends. Julie was just the girl Ann had wanted. She knew immediately they were kindred spirits.

"Who are the folks in the other wagons? Do you know all of them?" Ann questioned.

"Well, almost all of them. My Aunt Dorothy and Uncle Dean Emerson are in the wagon right behind Doc.

Ann: 1833-1897

Elizabeth is their oldest, then comes Claude. They're both older than Chuckie and me. Then the little boys, Mike and Marc, are 9 and 6.

The girls walked down the line of wagons.

Stopping, Julie said, "Now here behind Aunt Dorothy and Uncle Dean is my Aunt Rachel and Uncle Orren Maguire. With them are my cousins, Linnie, Eugene, and Rollie. They're almost grown.

"Uncle Orren brought two wagons. The boys tend to one, and Uncle Orren takes care of the other. That way he could bring more of his carpenter tools and equipment. Aunt Rachel wanted to bring along her small piano, but at the last minute she decided not to. Maybe she can send for it later. She and Uncle Orren are very musical. They like to sing a lot.

"Well, that's it. Seems as if our whole family decided to stay together, pull up stakes and move west."

"I wish some of my relatives had decided to come," said Ann, "'specially my grandpa. But he said he was too old to travel."

"My grandparents are dead. In fact, I don't remember my grandpa too much. When I was 5, my grandma drown—" But Julie did not finish the sentence. Instead she changed the subject. "You'll like my cousin Linnie," she said brightly. "Ma says she's as sweet as the day is long, and I think she's pretty. Gene and Rollie are proud of her, and they tell her she has to check with them before she even thinks of getting married! Gene is a big tease, and Rollie's fun, too." Julie sounded proud of her cousins.

Ann Makes a Friend

"Then Gene and Rollie will like our neighbor, Pete," Ann told her. "People say he's full of the ol' Nick. He's fun, too. They ought to get along well."

Julie turned around and taking Ann by the hand, she began walking back toward the front of the line. She said, "In that last wagon were the Westons. I'm not sure who they are, but Mr. Hathaway told my pa that they asked to come along at the last minute. Pa says that their two boys act like hooligans. Chuckie and me have orders to stay out of their way."

SIX

Wagons, Ho!

It took a while for everyone to mingle, meet, and greet one another. The men shook hands and slapped one another on the back. The women were gathered in a circle, and Ann could see them all talking at once.

This is fun. We're like one big family, Ann thought.

After giving everyone time to chat a bit, Mr. Hathaway called them together.

"Folks, I'm glad to have this opportunity to travel west with all of you. I've been over this trail many times before as a fur trapper and trader, and I'll do my best to lead you safely to your destination in a manner that will meet with your satisfaction."

Then he gave instructions and orders. He counseled the families about the rules for safety. He demanded their attention to the smallest detail, and he warned them about some of the dangers along the way and how they could handle emergencies. He spoke of snakes, wolves, and hailstorms.

Ann and Oscar listened in awe.

He sounds like a general . . .

I wonder if he knew George Washington . . .

Wagons, Ho!

I'm so glad he's been over this trail before . . .

All kinds of questions and thoughts flew through Ann's mind.

"This journey is not for cowards," the wagon master continued seriously, "but if we all follow orders, tend to business, watch out for the other fellow, and keep cool heads, with the help of the good Lord we'll do fine.

"At night when we stop, the wagons will be placed in a circle. My wagon will always be pointed toward the North Star, so we have our direction correct each morning. Animals will be tethered and hobbled so they won't wander off, and we'll set some of the men to watch and guard them. Children will play *inside* the circle—*not outside* of it. Remember that."

Mother looked knowingly at her children and raised her eyebrows as if to say, "Did you hear that? Stay inside the circle."

"Crossing rivers and creeks will take special care. Unless there's a ferry, we'll usually turn the animals free to swim across, and we'll float the wagons across.

"It's my purpose," he said, "to get you folks to your destination in time to raise a house and plant your late summer vegetables and crops before the cold weather sets in.

"Hawkeye will scout ahead to look for wolves, and will find a safe place to stop for the night. He will have us camp as close as possible to wood and water." He pointed to the man with the feather in his hair.

"Hawkeye has some Miami Indian blood in his veins. Traveled with me before, and I can tell you, he's good.

Ann: 1833-1897

He's savvy about the wilderness and animals and just about everything. But better not give him any trouble, because I know who'd win! He may not look exactly like an Indian, but I can tell you he knows how to fight like one. Everyone, meet Hawkeye," said Mr. Hathaway.

Just then Hawkeye's silver horse bucked and whinnied loudly. Everyone jumped with a start but then realized it was a trick that Hawkeye had trained his horse to do.

The crowd cheered and Hawkeye grinned widely.

He's friendly after all, Ann observed.

"Wow!" said Oscar. "What a horse!"

"Wow!" repeated Ozro.

"Next to Hawkeye is Luther St. John," Mr. Hathaway continued. The big man took off his coonskin hat and nodded his head. "Lute will bring up the rear and keep you all in line. If you have trouble, go to him or come and see me. A better man I've never met. Don't let his good looks fool you. He's tough and can make tough decisions in a flash. There's no one faster with a gun—fair warning. Each morning before sunrise, Lute will blow his bugle so you'll know it's time to get up. Folks, meet Lute."

Luther smartly saluted the crowd and raised his bugle over his head.

Everyone shouted, "Hey, Lute!" Erv stuck two fingers in his mouth and whistled loudly. Everyone clapped, and all the dogs barked.

Oscar tugged at his father's arm. "Ain't Lute's horse a beaut'—a Morgan! Someday I'll have me a Morgan horse."

"Me, too," said Ozro. "A Morgan."

Wagons, Ho!

"Well, that about does it," concluded Mr. Hathaway. "And if any of you have brought musical instruments, we'll have sing-alongs around the campfire at night for those that want to."

The folks murmured their consent and nodded their heads in agreement.

"Now before we begin this journey, let's all bow our heads and ask the good Father in heaven to protect and preserve us." The wagon master removed his hat, and all the men followed his example. Then lifting his face heavenward, Mr. Hathaway offered a short but sincere prayer.

"Aren't we fortunate to have a godly man in charge? It is providential that he's with us," Father said to Mother, and taking her arm they walked back to their wagon.

With her hand on Dixie's head, Ann and the boys followed their parents. By now all the dogs had met and greeted one another and established themselves. At first they had circled about each other, suspiciously wagging their tails. Some jumped and frisked about, others grumbled low in their throats, but no fighting occurred.

Everyone got busy, collected their children, checked on their livestock, and settled themselves. Mr. Hathaway went down the line, conferring with each family for any last minute questions.

Then climbing into his own wagon, Mr. Hathaway raised his gloved hand and shouted, "Forward, Hooooh!"

Everyone waved to those who came to see them off until they disappeared in the distance.

At last they were on their way!

SEVEN

First Day on the Trail

The Mohawk Trail was quite easy to see and follow, since it was old and well-traveled.

The sun shone brightly as the horses plodded along through the heavily wooded area. The blue sky and wispy white clouds made the day seem bright with hope for new opportunities.

Such a wonderful day, Ann thought.

Smiling at Julie walking along next to her, Ann was thankful to be alive for such an adventure.

Around noon they stopped to eat. Everyone was rather slow and awkward getting used to the new routine of preparing meals on the trail, and there was lots of fumbling clumsiness and laughs.

When the food was ready, the Eddy family bowed their heads and repeated their mealtime prayer:

"God is great, God is good,
    and we thank Him for this food.
By His goodness all are fed.
    Give us, Lord, our daily bread. Amen."

While they ate, Ann quietly told her parents that Mr.

First Day on the Trail

Hathaway scared her a little because he looked and sounded stern. Mother explained that a wagon master had to be alert, tough, exacting, and able to lead those under him in a safe and careful way.

"Your Pa says Hathaway was once a colonel in the army, so you best mind your step, children," admonished Mother.

Father nodded. "Yep, and his two scouts seem like rough and ready men. So I expect you to listen to them. I made it a point to speak to every new family in the train. We've a good bunch of people traveling with us, and I'm thankful.

"But I'm not sure about the Weston family," he added. "They aren't the friendliest bunch. They didn't even bother to talk to the rest of us much. You children stay out of their way. Hathaway says they're only going as far as Ohio somewhere."

Ann, Oscar, and even little Ozro listened intently.

"The boys swear like pirates, and they're rough with their horses," Oscar told the family in between bites. "And I saw one of the boys kick their dog."

"Well I never saw the likes, Oscar. You certainly have big ears and bright eyes," Mother said. "We haven't been on the road a day and you know all that already. Mind your pa and be careful, boy. There's no need to be rude—just careful. And remember how Grandpa always warned that children need to keep good company."

Oscar replied with a laugh, 'Oh yes, I know, 'birds of a feather flock together,' Grandpa loved that one—he said it often enough. I'll not forget it."

Ann: 1833-1897

"I won't forget it either," promised Ozro.

Father was pleased.

"I notice they've placed the Westons at the very end of the train," he said. "With Lute bringing up the rear, those boys won't dare misbehave or get out of line. He'll keep a close eye on them. Why, with one hand tied behind his back, Lute could whop any two of us at a time."

He turned for a quick glance along the row of wagons. "I'm grateful that Mr. Hathaway runs a tight ship. He won't tolerate any tom-foolery. Like your mother says, be careful, children."

"And you know what else?" Oscar asked softly so that no one eating nearby could hear him. "The mother Weston smokes a corncob pipe. I couldn't believe my eyes. It looks so funny."

Oscar rolled his eyes, and the children giggled quietly. Leave it to Oscar. He was always the one who paid attention to details. That's why Ann loved playing with him.

"Mind your manners," remarked Mother, and that was all she said.

Ann thought to herself, *Anyone who mistreats animals is no good. No good at all. And they better never ever kick Dixie.* It made her angry just to think of such a thing.

When Mr. Hathaway called a halt for the day, the wagons were circled just as he instructed. And when the evening meal was finished and all the chores were done, Mr. Hathaway gathered the folk around the center campfire. He

First Day on the Trail

praised them for their cooperation and answered questions that different people had. Then he told them, "This first night we're probably all too tired to do much activity, but it is my habit to always sing a hymn and say an evening prayer to close the day. Please join me in singing "A mighty fortress is our God," Martin Luther's wonderful hymn. I'm sure we all know that." He put his fiddle under his chin.

Ann thought that the singing sounded beautiful there in the middle of nowhere with the setting sun's rays painting the clouds a lovely golden hue. The very air seemed filled with an atmosphere of quiet peacefulness. Everyone was ready to call it a day.

Ann and Oscar thought that it was a great adventure to sleep on blankets under the wagon with Dixie. That first night, all was clear and still. Only a chorus of insect sounds and the chirp of tree toads could be heard. Brilliant, glittering stars filled the sky overhead. Ann easily identified the Big Dipper with its curved handle.

Vividly she remembered the story Mama had told her many, many times about the wonderful night when the stars seemed to fall right out of the sky. Somehow she was certain that the great God in heaven who created the sun, the moon, and all the starry hosts would guard and guide them to their new home.

Good night, Father. Please keep us safe, and I thank Thee so much for Julie with the lovely green eyes. Amen.

So Ann fell asleep listening to the soft rise and fall of the men's voices as they sat and talked until only embers glowed in the fire.

EIGHT

Walking, Walking

At the first hint of daylight, the bugle sounded. Ann rolled over and rubbed her eyes.

At home she and Oscar were used to hearing their pa, a devout man, begin his duties at the break of day by vigorously singing:

> "Lord in the morning
> > Thou shalt hear my voice ascending high;
> To Thee will I direct my prayer,
> > to Thee lift up mine eye."

Although he had a rich baritone voice, Ann and Oscar often had wished he wouldn't use it so early in the mornings. But the sound of the bugle was something else—loud and startling!

Ann leaned over and nudged Oscar.

"I know, I know, I'm awake," he muttered. "I heard the trumpet."

"It's a bugle, silly."

So they rolled out of bed and did their chores without whining or complaining.

Oscar fed and watered the horses. He rubbed their

Walking, Walking

noses and talked to them, and they snorted and whinnied back, just as if they knew what he was saying.

Ozro learned to shake out the blankets in the fresh air, then with Ann's help fold them neatly and put them away.

Father milked Pansy.

Mother started the fire and began beating the batter for flapjacks. Ann stirred and stirred the cornmeal mush and kept an eye on it so it wouldn't burn.

"I declare, Annie, you're turning out to be a marvelous little cook," Mother told her daughter as she watched her tend the mush. "Why, when I was your age my mama despaired at my cooking skills. She said that I couldn't boil water without burning it."

They both laughed, and Ann couldn't help but feel a little surge of pride as her mother gave her a smile of approval.

"This camping is kind-a fun, Mama, but it's inconvenient, too—not like at home with our big fireplace and all the dishes, pots, and pans so handy."

"You're right about that, Ann, but I 'spect we'll get used to it. This won't be an easy journey, by any means, but never fear, we'll make it."

When they finished eating, Mother showed Ann how to scrub the plates with sand to clean them, then she rinsed them with water. "Today I want you and Oscar to help Ozro gather sticks for firewood," she said. "But take care that Ozro learns not to stray too far away. I don't want him lost in that tall prairie grass." Mother looked quite serious as she gave these instructions.

I wonder if the Pilgrims had it this difficult, Ann thought.

Ann: 1833-1897

She'd learned about the famous voyage of the *Mayflower* to Plymouth in the New World 200 years before. Grandpa had told them of their own pilgrim ancestor, Samuel Eddy, who had sailed from England on the *Handmaid* to Plymouth Colony in 1630.

Gradually the wagon train travel became routine. Everyone learned to adapt and adjust so that life became somewhat easier, although walking was painful. Especially during the first several days, it wasn't unusual to see folks limping because of their sore feet. Often after supper Ann saw three or four people soaking their tired feet in warm water they'd carried from the creek and heated over the campfire. However sore their limbs would be, walking was still better than riding in the bumpy, jerking wagon. Even the children used walking sticks, and sleep came easy every night.

Ann and Julie walked together whenever they could and shared their time getting better acquainted. Ann noticed that Julie's cousin, Elizabeth Emerson, was quite taken with all the younger children. "She plans to become a teacher," Julie said.

Elizabeth, it seemed, never walked by herself. She always had Ozro, Mike, Marc, Thelma, and Agnes with her. They seemed attracted to her like bees to the summer flowers. Elizabeth was bright and clever at teaching them words and numbers, and it helped her and the children to pass the time as the journey continued.

Walking, Walking

"It's a relief not to have Thelma sticking to me," sighed Ann to herself. "Now she has someone else to look up to."

"Mama, why doesn't it bother Elizabeth to have the little ones follow her around?" Ann asked one morning.

"You'll have to realize, my girl, that Elizabeth is older than you are, so she sees the children in a different way."

※

Some days Ann carried young Nancy to give Nellie a break. When she became heavy Ann held her hand and walked with her a while. Nellie appreciated all the help she could get for her two boys took up much of her time. They were the "babies" of the train. Herb was rather frail, but Erv mentioned to Mother and Father one day, "You know, I do believe all this fresh air and exercise is good for Herb. He's still scrawny, but his energy and strength has improved greatly. He rarely rides with me anymore. He often wants to walk." Erv grinned, looking across at his older son who walked out of earshot. "His color has improved, too. Nellie and I are delighted. We've both noticed how active he's becoming. 'Course, Linnie Maguire visits with Nellie a lot, and young Herb has taken quite a liking to her. That relieves Nellie of some of her work."

"Are you sure Linnie's visits don't have something to do with Pete?" Father had a twinkle in his eye.

Erv pushed his hat back and chuckled. "You could be right. Pete has never been backward in becoming acquainted with people, but he seems a bit shy around Linnie."

Ann: 1833-1897

"Give him enough time, and I suppose that will change." They laughed together.

Ann was grateful that Mr. Hathaway always gave them a short rest after the noontime meal. Not a long rest, but enough to catch their breath. She often saw him watch the sky as he walked up and down the wagon train checking if all was in order.

During one noon break, Julie flopped down on the grass next to Ann. She picked up the bonnet that Ann had taken from her head and placed on the ground. "My ma and Aunt Dorothy are seamstresses, and they hope to have a little shop of their own in the new land. I like to sew, too, and Ma says I have true sewing fingers." She ran a finger around the brim of the bonnet. "Ma told me that my fingers are made for sewing. She says that I'm better at tiny, straight stitches than she was at my age. I make all my own bonnets."

"I'm not much for bonnets. They make me feel smothered," Ann told her. "I'd rather wear an old straw hat to keep the sun off my nose, and sometimes I don't even wear that!"

They both laughed. Ann's nose was a little sunburned, and despite the sunbonnet her face was growing tanned. "Maybe some day if we don't live too far from each other, I'll make you a pretty calico dress," Julie said. "In fact, I'll make a matching one for myself. Then we can look like twins." Her green eyes twinkled. "Maybe I'll even become famous, and people will come to me from all over just to have me make them a stylish gown."

Walking, Walking

Just a few yards away Chuckie was talking to Oscar. He seemed to take a special liking to the boy, despite the age difference between them. Both of the boys loved horses. When Oscar told him that he often helped his pa shoe horses back at home, Chuckie replied, "So that's why you're so good handling horses."

"Guess so. Sometimes I pumped the bellows for Papa in the blacksmith shop, too. It blew air and fanned the flames to make the fire hotter."

"Did ya ever get burned?" asked Chuckie, wide-eyed.

"Not too bad, though once I dropped a hot coal on my shoe and it burned a hole clean through to my toe."

"Ow! That must uv been a scorcher!" Both boys laughed.

"I jumped like a jack rabbit and stuck my foot in a bucket of water. Another time I touched a hot anvil. Yoww! I was good 'n' careful after that. But I liked helping to shoe horses best."

NINE

Making Music

In the evenings, after Mr. Hathaway's devotional time, folks sat around the campfire and visited—that is, everyone except the Westons. There was always plenty of lively music. Talented Dean Emerson played both the banjo and the fiddle. Some others plucked their guitars. Others twanged on jew's harps or puffed their harmonicas. Lute blew on an empty water jug, making a hollow rhythmic sound. Hawkeye beat on a kettle with a mallet just like it was an Indian tom-tom.

As soon as the music began, everyone, both young and old, started to clap and sing. Some would even grab a partner and dance.

Doc Willoughby and Dawson Dunbar were the show stoppers. Doc tootled away on his fife and even yodeled, much to the children's delight. But they loudly clapped, cheered, and laughed when Doc and Dawson danced a lively jig. Soon all the youngsters were trying to dance along with them.

"You know," said Mr. Hathaway, "this is the most talented bunch I've ever seen in my life. Let's do Turkey in the Straw, and everyone sing along." And sing they did, with pleasure, delight, and amusement.

Making Music

Sometimes Oscar and Pete got so caught up in the fun that they'd do a cartwheel or two while the group was singing and dancing. Or they would walk on their hands and turn cartwheels together—one right after the other.

Eugene and Rollie were amazed at the stunts. Now and then they tried to walk on their hands, but it was difficult at first. Claude and Chuckie wanted in on the fun, too, so Pete gave instructions to all four of them, and they had a good time practicing.

Now I see why Pete calls Oscar a natural. He just seems to know where to put his hands and feet, and he has such a good sense of balance. Ann was proud of her lithe and limber brother.

Lute enjoyed watching the circus, as he called it. Pete urged him to try, but Lute said he was only "as graceful as the bird they call the elephant," so he declined the offer.

Rachel and Orren Maguire often sang together. The folks enjoyed hearing them. Mrs. Russell loved songs from old Ireland, and she would often ask Orren to sing her favorite, "Danny Boy." With Dean Emerson and Mr. Hathaway playing their fiddles while he sang, the music was both sweet and sad. Ann couldn't help notice that Mrs. Russell wiped her eyes with a hankie whenever he sang.

"Good Irish tenors always sing with a tear in their voice," Mrs. Russell smilingly explained. "That makes me have a tear in my eye." And Ann understood in her young heart just what Mrs. Russell meant.

There was something about music that fed Ann's soul. From the time she was very young, she could harmonize when songs were sung. No one had to teach her. She just knew which notes sounded right together.

Back home in New York, Ann and Oscar sometimes sang in church, but now Oscar didn't want anyone to know he sang. "But you have a good voice," Ann had said. He grinned but told her not to mention it, at least not right away.

There were two folk songs that Mr. Maguire sang that Ann liked best—"The Lass of Richmond Hill" and "Mairi's Wedding." After hearing them a couple times, she had memorized the words and would sing quietly along with him to herself.

> "This lass so neat with smiles so sweet
>   has won my right goodwill.
> I'd crowns resign to call her mine,
>   Sweet Lass of Richmond Hill . . ."

Mr. Maguire held the note just a bit when he sang the word, 'mine,' and looked at his wife with a sparkle in his eye. Mrs. Maguire would coyly smile and look away, but even the children knew she loved the song and her husband.

When he sang the lively "Mairi's Wedding," the folks would tap their toes.

> "Step we gaily on we go,
>   Heel for heel and toe for toe-oh,
> Arm in arm and on we go,
>   All for Mairi's wedding . . ."

Julie and Ann noticed that Pete usually found a way

Making Music

to sit next to Linnie during the evenings, and they girlishly giggled quietly about it. They figured he was sweet on the attractive, young lady.

"Pete better watch his step," Julie whispered. Ann knew she was thinking of Rollie and Gene keeping track of their sister's activities and potential beaus.

Some evenings the young people—all except the Weston boys—would sit away from the older folk telling tales, singing, and laughing. They played rhyming games and guessing games, told riddles, and made up stories.

One of their favorite amusements was to follow along with Chuckie when he'd start a funny word game. These games went something like this:

"This morning I saw an old, dead skunk. I *one* him . . . ," Chuckie would begin.

And then those in the circle would humorously be obliged to take their turn counting.

"I *two* him," came next. Then, "I *three* him." The counting continued until the last unlucky person had to say, "I *eight* him!"

Everyone hoped it would not be his turn to say he "ate" the old, dead skunk.

Ann stumped everyone one night with a riddle:

> "Two ducks ahead of a duck.
> Two ducks behind a duck.
> And one duck in the middle.
> How many ducks can you count?"

Julie promptly hollered out, "Five!"

Ann: 1833-1897

But Ann said, "Wrong!" They all looked puzzled, so she explained, "The answer is *three*. Add them up for yourself. Put up three fingers of one hand and count—two in front, two behind, and one in the center.

What a good laugh they had as they groaned at their own slowness in not catching the trick question.

Elizabeth chuckled. "Now that's a good one, Ann, I'll not forget it. I'll trick my students with it someday when I'm a teacher."

"I'm gonna get you for that, young lady," Claude vowed with laughter. "Just you wait and see!"

"I'll help you think of somethin', Claude," threatened Chuckie with a comical scowl at Ann.

Julie playfully leaned on Ann making her fall over in the grass for causing them to feel dumb and dull-witted, but Ann didn't care—she just giggled, pointed her finger at the group and exclaimed, "Got'cha!"

※

The days came and went. They awoke to the bugle and early morning haze. After breakfast the wagons started their slow rolling. They saw no farms or houses or any signs of people. The only difference Ann noticed as she walked along was the occasional change in scenery—from heavy woods to a grassy meadow here and there. She thought they looked like huge flower gardens with their pink verbena, bluebells, and wild indigo. Mr. Hathaway pointed out the tall buckeye chestnut trees with their large leaves. Ann had not seen them before.

Making Music

The wagons squeaked and rolled over the trail which gradually became just two long lines of wheel tracks with here and there a tree stump. There would be an occasional cracking of the whips when the men called commands to their horses on the endless, dusty road.

And there was always the tinkling of the cow bells, the constant thudding of hooves, and the grunting and mooing of the herds.

"The animals are all doing quite well, I feel, and for that I'm thankful," Father mentioned one day.

Oscar spoke up. "All the animals 'cept Weston's dog. Chuckie and I feed him scraps sometimes when no one is looking. He's a pitiful sight, he is. I don't know why they even have a dog. They pay no 'tention to him at all. He just walks along every day with his head down and his tail dragging."

"Well, you boys are kinder to him than his owners, but be careful that you don't aggravate that family."

Rarely did they meet any Indians, but a few times friendly ones came along—some with buffalo robes to trade for any goods the travelers had. But generally they just rode by on their horses.

The children were in awe of them.

"Will they hurt us, Papa?" Ozro was worried.

"I don't believe they will. Remember that all men are brothers. I recall hearing that William Penn made it a point to treat the Indians fair and square. That's what we should all do."

TEN

Trouble

Most of the time the weather was remarkably pleasant. Even Mr. Hathaway said so. But there were miserable days, too, and Ann couldn't decide which were more wretched—hot, dry days or sloppy, rainy ones.

On hot, dry days the trail smelled like hot animals and hot animal droppings. At times Ann gagged at the stench—and the flies swarming over it.

Mother had them use bandanas to keep the dust out of their mouths and eyes. To get away from the dust, they walked through the grass at the edge of the trail.

The hot weather caused some of the wagon wheels to shrink and crack. When that happened the iron rims would loosen and fall off. Mr. Hathaway told Father he was always grateful when a blacksmith traveled with him—someone who could repair the rims, grease the wheel hubs, or reshoe the horses so that the wagons could roll as soon as possible.

One day as Father worked on a cracked wheel with Pete and Erv, Mr. Hathaway confided, "Those Westons are a strange lot. The boys are lazy, and the man's not much better. Both Lute and Hawkeye are watchful and wary of them. The whole family stays at a distance, but that's fine by me, just so's they mind what they're doing and don't cause trouble." He made a face. "They do make me feel uneasy, though."

Father agreed. "I've warned the children to stay clear of them, and so far they've minded."

"You've got good kids, Willard," said Pete. "You're a lucky man. I hope to have nice kids someday."

"So we've noticed, Pete," teased Erv. "Seems like you've set your cap for some young lady already." He grabbed Pete's hat and laughing, tossed it in the air.

"Are you blushing, Pete?" Father joked.

"Ah, go on, you fellas," was Pete's good-natured reply, but he looked a little embarrassed.

There were days when Ozro was bored. "Annie, make me laugh," he'd beg, so she'd get in the wagon with him and they'd play games like I Spy. Sometimes she'd sing-song funny little sayings to him. She taught him to spell "Mississippi" by repeating, M-I-crooked letter-crooked letter-I-

Crooked letter-crooked letter-I-

Humpback-humpback-I

Other times he'd ask, "Say some tongue twisters, Annie." So Ann would rapidly repeat the two twisters he liked best.

"Whether the weather be fine,
or whether the weather be not

Ann: 1833-1897

Whether the weather be cold,
    or whether the weather be hot
We'll weather the weather
    whatever the weather
Whether we like it or not."

Then there was this one:

"How much wood would a woodchuck chuck,
    if a woodchuck could chuck wood?
He'd chuck as much wood as a woodchuck could,
    if a woodchuck could chuck wood."

Ozro would laugh and try to repeat them, and beg her to say them again. Sometimes they'd sing. Ozro's little voice was clear and sweet. If Julie heard them, she'd climb in the wagon to listen. But it was so hot under the canvas and such a bumpy ride they didn't stay in the wagon for very long.

ELEVEN

Toby Gets Hurt

One day Mr. Hathaway called a halt so that Father could look at one of Henry Russell's horses. It had started to limp and Mr. Hathaway never ignored any sign of injury. "Better to be careful than sorry," he'd say.

Some of the fellows went for a quick hunt in the woods. It was a quiet, still day, and they wanted to see what they might find.

Mother and Rachel Maguire had gone to get fresh water. Everyone seemed to be occupied doing one thing or another. Ann and Julie were visiting with Elizabeth. The younger ones were resting.

Since there was nothing else to do, Oscar walked around by himself, picking up nuts from a nearby hickory tree. All of a sudden one of the Weston boys called to him. "Hey there, kid. Come show me how to do a flip."

Forgetting his parents' warnings, he walked back to their wagon. Dixie followed him unnoticed. Oscar did a flip or two, and the Weston boys laughed and slapped their knees.

"Wow, you're good! Now do a cartwheel."

Next they asked him to stand on his head. He chose a

Ann: 1833-1897

level spot of grass, placed his head and hands securely and squarely on the ground, and slowly raised his feet. Quick as a flash, Edgar booted him in the seat of his pants and knocked him over. Then both Weston boys laughed uproariously, elbowing each other.

"Whats-a-matter kid? Can't you get up?" Toby teased.

Bewildered, Oscar tried to get up, but when Edgar started to give him another kick, Oscar saw it coming. Quick as a wink, he grabbed the boy's leg and gave it a yank and a twist. In a second, Edgar was down on the ground, momentarily knocked breathless. Oscar jumped to his feet.

"Why you little divil, you," yelled Toby starting toward him.

But the Weston boys had definitely underestimated Dixie. Dixie's dog instinct told him that Oscar was being hurt. In a flash Dixie became a blur of black fur, growling, snarling, and barking.

He was everywhere! First he lunged at Toby knocking him to the ground. Then he turned on Edgar who was trying to back away. Dixie grabbed him by the pant leg and began pulling.

There was no time for the Weston boys to run.

Back at their wagon, Ann heard a commotion and noticed the skirmish down at the Weston's wagon. She yelled, "Oscar! Oscar! Dixie! Dixie! Papa! Papa!"

Father came on the run, and right behind him was Lute who immediately sized up the situation. In an instant, Lute had grabbed the two boys. One tried to take a

Toby Gets Hurt

swing at him, but got nowhere—Lute was as big and as strong as two men. Taking the boys by their collars, he marched them over to their wagon.

Standing in front of Mr. Weston, Lute said, "I don't know exactly what happened here, Homer Weston, but you must have seen the scuffle. Why didn't you put a stop to it?"

Mr. Weston shrugged his shoulders and spat a stream of tobacco juice off to the side of the wagon.

Glaring at the boys, Lute bellowed, "Either of you boys want to take a punch at me rather than picking on Oscar? Come on, put 'em up, I'm ready for you." Lute was angry.

The boys made no move.

"What's-a-matter, fellas? Are you all tuckered out?" he taunted.

The boys lowered their heads and said nothing.

Mr. Hathaway had by now joined the group, and to the father he said, "So help me, Homer Weston, if I ever hear of your boys trying to hurt any other children in this wagon train again—let alone getting anywhere near them—you will be forced to leave and finish the journey by yourself."

Lute went over to Father who was holding Oscar close with one arm. With the other he hung on to Dixie who was still growling and grumbling.

Then they all walked away.

"Whatever got into that head o' yours to go near those boys?" Lute asked Oscar. "Stay away from them. You were lucky Dixie came along when he did. Why, I would have liked to have had a tussle with 'em myself to show them a thing or two, but Dixie did it for me. Now then, ya' stay clear of them, ya' hear me?"

Oscar nodded. He wasn't badly hurt at all, but his pride was wounded. He knew he had disappointed his parents, Lute, and Mr. Hathaway.

"You know, Willard," Mr. Hathaway confided, "it won't be long now and they'll be leaving the train. They're only going as far as the middle of Ohio, so I 'spose that's why Homer Weston seemed not to be disturbed. Good riddance, I say."

Mother's arms encircled Oscar. "Are you all right, son?"

Oscar nodded again, sheepishly.

Lute patted Oscar's head, and Father shook Lute's hand.

"Thanks, Lute."

"The thanks go to Dixie," Lute replied.

Oscar quite willingly remained in Mother's embrace for a moment.

"I'd like to punch that Edgar Weston right in the nose!" exclaimed Chuckie who'd returned from hunting with the other men.

"Thanks, Chuckie, but we've had enough fighting for one day," Father said with a little smile. "Let's all get back to our business now."

Ann and Ozro were filled with loving sympathy for their brother. They hugged him and asked if he hurt anywhere. Ann got him a drink of water, and Ozro put his arm around Oscar's neck.

Toby Gets Hurt

Mother had Oscar get into the wagon.

"Oh, Mama, I can walk. I'm really all right." He was more humbled than tired.

But Mother insisted that all three children ride with her for a while. Smoothing Oscar's tousled hair, she gently said, "Now, son, I want you to be quiet and think. It was wrong of the boys to hit you, but it was wrong of you to go anywhere near them when we'd asked you not to. So just quietly ponder this experience and the consequences of disobedience. Think what might have happened. You could have a broken arm or leg as a result—or worse. I thank God for His protection."

Father put Dixie up on the seat beside him, just to know where he was. And once again the wagon train was on its way.

After a bit, Ozro fell asleep snuggled next to Oscar. When Ann saw that her brother was really not seriously harmed, she smiled at him, then jumped out and walked with Julie. Mother hummed while she knitted, and soon Oscar himself, rather exhausted after all the commotion, slept in spite of the bumpy ride.

The news about the row caused the travelers some uneasiness, but Mr. Hathaway put a stop to any muttered threats or complaints. "Those are troublesome boys, but they're marked boys now," was all he would say. So by his deliberate, level-headed, diplomatic handling of the situation, life returned to normal.

The next day was hot again, but along in the afternoon the sky suddenly went from bright blue to dark

Ann: 1833-1897

black. The breeze changed to a strong wind that swirled around them, blowing specks of dirt into their eyes and lifting their hats off their heads. Mr. Hathaway excitedly shouted the order for the wagon train to halt. No one had to be urged twice. All obeyed immediately. The wind blew ferociously. Canvas covers billowed and flapped so hard that folks feared they would rip.

When at last the wind died down, rain fell like a giant waterfall. Lightning sizzled in the air. Thunder rumbled like the voice of deep, loud drums. The storm spooked the cattle and horses, and they were hard to control. Everyone—men, women, and children—scrambled to their wagons to wait it out. There was not much anyone could do in the terrible torrent of rain.

Ann was with Julie in the Dunbar wagon, and through the pelting rain they saw a sorry sight. Edgar and Toby Weston tried to jump into the wagon with their folks, but Mr. Weston stuck out his foot and pushed the boys away, at the same time shaking his fist at them. So the boys slid under their wagon where they'd have some cover at least, but it was not dry there by any means. Streams of water ran under every wagon.

Helen Dunbar had seen it all. "No wonder those boys behave like ruffians and bullies. Their pa is despicable. And you know, if a man's wicked, he can't keep the wickedness out of his face anymore than a good man can hide his goodness. I think that's why Homer Weston's face looks so pinched and pained."

"Well, he certainly doesn't understand the Bible's

Toby Gets Hurt

Golden Rule. In Matthew 7:12 we're told to do unto others as we would have them do unto us. I've read that text for myself," Ann remarked.

The Dunbars looked at Ann with admiration and approval.

"You seem to be acquainted with the Scriptures. We hear your family pray before each meal, and it's a habit we are going to establish in our home from now on." Helen was serious, and Dawson nodded and said he certainly agreed.

The rain and storm ended by evening. Firewood was so soaked that it was difficult to get fires started. At last, here and there, a few fires weakly began to burn. Everyone, young and old, gathered round trying to dry out. As they talked about the hard rain they'd just had, Chuckie told the young folks how his parents got word the year before from family members who'd been in a wagon train going to Illinois.

"My cousin Tom said that when they traveled from Tennessee to Illinois it rained 'most constantly, making their trip really hard. There were only a few bridges, and after crossing the Ohio River the streams were so swollen by all the rain that the men were awful troubled.

"There was a ferry for crossing of the Wabash River, but the cattle wouldn't stay on the boat. Those cows jumped off the ferry and swam back to the bank. Can you imagine it? The men took off their outer clothes, got into the water and grabbed the cattle by their tails. And the men guided those ole' cows across the river. Swam them

Ann: 1833-1897

across. Tom swam the Wabash 11 times!"

"You're full of malarkey, Chuckie, I don't believe ya." Oscar was flabbergasted. "How could anyone swim the river a'leven times?" He shook his head in disbelief.

"No, he's telling the truth." Claude supported his cousin's incredible story.

"Lute says we'll be crossing the Maumee River one of these days. I know there's a ferry there, and I can't help but think about those cattle and Tom," said Chuckie.

Ann had listened intently. She remembered how she and Oscar had both learned to swim in Butterfield's pond back home. And she recalled how they'd swing from a tree limb and drop into the water with a huge splash. It was fun, but she just could not picture that Tom fellow swimming so long and hard across a swollen river.

Ann was grateful she knew how to swim. She thought of Mrs. Abernathy who'd lived down the road from their farm back in New York....

"Willard Eddy," the lady had scolded Ann's father, "it's indecent for girls to be in the water. They have no business swimming."

"Mrs. Abernathy," he patiently replied, "there's nothing disgraceful about it. I intend to teach all my children to swim. It might someday save their lives."

Mother stood firmly behind Father in his decision. "Mrs. Abernathy is a fuddy-duddy," Mother said to Ann in disgust. "That's what she is. Pay no mind to what she says. Your pa is not wrong in this."

I wonder if Mrs. Abernathy would think it was indecent

Toby Gets Hurt

for the men and Tom to have taken off their clothes in order to swim easier in the Wabash River when they saved the cattle. Ann couldn't help smiling to herself.

The next day the weather turned sunny, but the ground was still too wet for traveling. The wagon wheels sank into the mud. The Emerson's discovered they had a broken axle, and Ted Grant noticed that one of his wheels was loose and about to come off. This repair had to be done before the journey could continue. Mr. Hathaway said they had to wait until the ground was drier before they traveled again, so people took advantage of the delay and aired their clothing and bedding and reorganized their wagons. They lifted the flaps of the canvas covers to let in the air so it could circulate and help remove the dampness. Father and some of the other men helped Dean Emerson, and then they worked on the Grant's wheel.

Ann and Oscar went down to the creek to get water so their mother could do some much needed laundry. As they neared the bank, they heard a moaning sound. What was it? They walked slower and stopped talking so they could hear better. There it was again. Then up ahead they saw a fallen tree. Approaching carefully, they saw Toby Weston on the ground covered by twigs and branches. His face was bloodied from a cut on his forehead and he twisted in pain. Even before they got to him the children saw that his leg was caught underneath the branch of a tree. He didn't seem to notice them but kept on groaning and moaning, "Help, help. Someone please help me."

Immediately, Ann and Oscar rushed to his side. Toby opened his eyes and looked helplessly at them.

"Toby, what happened? Did you fall down?" they asked.

Toby took a deep breath. "I hardly remember. Thought I'd catch me some fish, so I was here alone, mindin' me own business . . . when I heard a giant creak and crackle—" he took a breath and the children saw he was crying.

"Take your time, Toby," Ann said softly. She looked at Oscar and he pointed upward with his chin. They both stared at the big tree where a slash of lightning had struck and splintered a limb during the bad storm. The limb had eventually worked loose and landed on Toby.

"What shall we do, Annie?"

"Shall we run for help?" she asked.

"No, no, please don't leave me," Toby begged. "I'm afraid I'll die." He kept talking to keep them there. "I looked around to see what the noise was, and before I knew it I slid in the wet grass and fell down . . . and the pain in my leg was like fire. Aah, ah, ooooo, ouch, ouch," he groaned.

Without more delay, Ann and Oscar started pulling away the twigs and branches that were scattered around Toby. They knew they'd have to do something to free him if they could.

Catching his breath Toby sobbed, "Just then this branch from that tree fell . . . with a big whoosh. I couldn't move fast enough, though I managed to roll away some. Oww, oww . . . my leg! The branch fell right across

Toby Gets Hurt

my knee," he gasped, ". . . and pinned me down. The pain was so fierce, I think I went blank. When I came to I feared a bobcat or wolf would git me if no one found me!" He jerked from side to side with pain. "Finally, I heard voices and started calling for help. When I opened my eyes, there you were. Please help me. Ooooooooo, ooowww! Please do something. Hurry! Hurry!" And his eyes closed again in miserable pain.

Ann and Oscar tried pulling and pushing on the branch that held Toby's leg down, but he groaned with every move they made. So they started digging in the mud and dirt with their hands and with sticks and stones.

"If we can just get enough dirt out from under his leg, mebbe then he can move it," Oscar muttered. They dug rapidly, sensing the urgency. Neither Ann nor Oscar knew if they were really doing the right thing, but there was nothing else to do. The log was too big for them to lift.

Toby felt the dirt give way, and he gave a loud groan. The children helped him move his leg just far enough to free it from under the heavy limb.

"Oh, that's better, that's better," he stammered. He tried getting up but was not able to put any weight on it at all.

"Now that your leg is free, we'll run for Doc Willoughby. He'll know what to do," Oscar told him.

"No! Please don't leave me," Toby pleaded, but Ann was off in a flash. She was shaking from head to foot.

And I'm not the one who was hurt! she thought with a shudder.

Ann: 1833-1897

Mother saw Ann come running without Oscar with her. "Oh, no," she gasped covering her mouth in disbelief, and fear. *What's happened now?*

"Mama, where's Doc Willoughby? Toby's leg is broken, and Oscar stayed with him, so's he wouldn't faint again," Ann breathlessly explained.

Mother stared at Ann. Then coming to her senses, she grabbed Ann's hand and together they ran for Doc Willoughby.

Ann couldn't remember every detail of what happened after that, but she did lead the doctor, Mr. Hathaway, and Lute back to poor Toby. Mother went to the Weston wagon and told the parents the few details she knew. Then she and several others ran to the creek. Toby was taken carefully to Doc Willoughby's wagon. The kindly doctor set the boys leg, cleaned him up, and put him to bed in his own wagon.

"You just stay with me a couple of days so I can keep an eye on you, Toby. This makeshift splint will have to do." The doctor patted Toby's arm. "But you're going to be alright, my boy. The tree didn't break your leg," he explained. "It only held you there on the ground. You broke your leg when you twisted and fell. So you need to stay with me these first few days." He looked down on the boy. "And don't worry about that cut on your head. It'll heal fine."

Mrs. Weston came hobbling on her cane to see how Toby was. Ann had never seen much of her, and was surprised to see she was crippled.

The small, bent woman approached Ann and Oscar

Toby Gets Hurt

with sad eyes. "Thankee, you young'uns, for helpin' poor Toby. I'm mighty obliged to ya' all." And with those few but important words, she limped back to her wagon.

Just before supper, Edgar came to Doc's wagon carrying a large pheasant over one shoulder and his gun over the other. "Ma sent me a-huntin' and I caught this for ya', Doc." He handed the bird to the rather surprised doctor who thanked him for the gift.

Peeking in on Toby, Edgar said, "'Tis a pity, li'l brother. Hurry 'n git well. I'll miss 'ya."

Doc was rather surprised but grateful to see any slight display of affection between the boys. "I didn't think they had it in them," he muttered to himself more than to anyone else.

Two days later, the wagon train was underway once again. One long day followed another, and everyone grew weary. Ann was tired of eating beef jerky and dried apples, and nuts. Everyone got tired of eating the same old thing. She even dreamed of regular food—especially apple pie like they had back home!

Home? she thought. *We left home behind.*

Pete took Ozro and Oscar fishing with him from time to time. A fish to eat was at least a break from the routine.

Walking mile after mile, day after day, people's feet got sore. By now many were limping. Often after supper, several soaked their tired feet in water they'd hauled from a stream.

"The only fun thing to do is go for water," complained Ann to Julie. "But if the creek or river is too far away, my folks won't let me go."

Ann: 1833-1897

"I know," replied Julie. "Same here."

Once when the girls were allowed to go to the river, they saw some Indians paddling a canoe. They waved a greeting, and the Indians waved back. "Wait 'till we tell the folks about this!" they said.

TWELVE

Independence Day

"Surprise!" said Mr. Hathaway after supper one night. "Day after tomorrow is Independence Day, so let's take that day off and celebrate."

Everyone thought that was a splendid idea. The women planned ahead and cooked like they hadn't cooked before. By using some of the food they'd been saving, they baked treats—pies and cookies. The men helped where they could and everyone's spirits were lifted.

When the morning of the fourth of July arrived, Lute blew his bugle differently—with the hint of a tune. They all got up laughing at how funny it sounded.

Mr. Hathaway had hung an American flag from his wagon. It looked so good to the travelers. They felt refreshed by the change in pace. Today they'd relax! Independence Day needed to be remembered, to be observed. It was a good time to count their blessings. Most everyone dressed themselves in clean clothes, and their hearts were filled with joy.

"Necessity is the mother of invention," Helen Dunbar said to Mother as they cooked side by side. "I didn't know I could cook so good with so little." They laughed together.

Ann: 1833-1897

By noon there was trout to eat and baked potatoes with gravy, corn, pheasant, and berries. The women used all their ingenuity to try to cook something different.

Tablecloths were spread, and the folk ate heartily.

After the dinner had been cleared away and the camp tidied up, everyone sat down to visit and to simply lounge. Elizabeth helped the children plan games and races, and she even arranged a parade, including the dogs.

After a while, Mr. Hathaway surprised everyone by asking for their attention and pulling out a rather dog-eared piece of paper.

When things became quiet, he said, "I am going to read a short portion of the second paragraph of the Declaration of Independence, something which rings true and warms every American heart. This was given to me by my grandfather in his own handwriting, and every year or so I make myself a new copy of this section to assure myself that I will never lose it." He smiled and then proceeded slowly and deliberately:

"We hold these truths to be self-evident: that all men are created equal; that they are endowed by their Creator with certain inalienable rights; that among these are life, liberty, and the pursuit of happiness . . .

"And that, my friends, is what we as a people are all about. Do you agree?"

Lute threw his hat into the air. Gene and Rollie whistled. And everyone cheered, "Hip, hip, hooray!"

The kids jumped up and down, laughing and hollering. When the clamor died, everyone sat back down.

Independence Day

Orren and Rachel, with Mother and Father, sang "Ash Grove" and "Annie Laurie."

"With some practice, we'd be good," laughed Father.

"You're good without practice," Dean Emerson complimented them.

Out of the blue, Mrs. Russell suggested that Ann and Oscar sing for the grownups. "I've heard you sing in church back home. Come, now, sing us a song." She smiled brightly at Ann.

Ann hesitated, looked at Oscar who was looking the other way, then she looked at her mother. Mother shrugged her shoulders. "Why not, children? Maybe 'Pop, Goes the Weasel.'"

Ozro pulled at Ann's arm. "Come on, I'll sing with you."

Ann pulled at Oscar's arm. So all three got up. Ann gave them the note and they started. The more they sang, the more the people nodded to the time. Ozro would call out "Pop!" so enthusiastically that everyone laughed. Even Oscar got less bashful as people's eyes were on Ozro.

"More, more!" shouted the crowd. So next they sang, "Yankee Doodle." Everyone joyfully joined in at the end, and clapped long and loud when the children finished.

"One more, please?" called out Julie.

Oscar had already plopped down on the grass, but Ann pulled on his arm and whispered in both his ear and in Ozro's. She gave the note again, and the three of them began softly singing the old familiar lullaby they loved so much:

Ann: 1833-1897

"Sleep, my child, and peace attend thee,
All through the night;
Guardian angels God will send thee,
All through the night...."

By the time they finished, something had happened to the crowd. It seemed hushed but overjoyed. It was a magical calm. Then the applause came, slowly at first, but increasing with exuberance.

"That was very good, children. Thanks. That song brought us serenity and peace," said Mr. Hathaway.

Mrs. Russell got out her hankie and dabbed at her eyes. "Beautiful, just beautiful," she said and pulled Ozro next to her. "That was beautiful, dearie. I didn't know you sang, too. Oh, oh . . ." She was overcome.

"That singing was food and nourishment for our souls." Mr. Maguire smiled his appreciation. "Did you and Hannah teach the children to sing, Willard?"

Father was glowing with pride and Mother's eyes sparkled.

"Yes, we sing a lot in our home, at church, at work, and at play," he replied. "The children come by it quite naturally."

Mrs. Maguire shook the boys' hands, then taking Ann's chin in her hand said, "I hope we live somewhere near each other when we all get settled in Wisconsin. I plan to send for my piano as soon as we have a home built. If you'd like to learn to play, I'll be happy to teach you. You are a talented little girl."

Independence Day

Ann could hardly believe her ears. "Oh, Mrs. Maguire, I'd love to learn. You're kind. Thank you!"

Then Mrs. Maguire sat down to talk to Mother and Father. Julie had overheard the conversation between Mrs. Maguire and Ann. She took Ann's arm. "Isn't that nice of her, Ann? You are lucky."

The folks got back to their celebrating and chatting and visiting. The day was comfortable, easy, and refreshing. It was a day that was sorely needed to give rest to the weary travelers, and it was a day Ann never forgot.

The next morning everyone went back to the routine of trudging along, mile after long mile. Some days they walked as much as 15 or 20 miles, other days only six. It all depended on the weather, the trail, and the condition of the animals. Day after day they felt a spirit of anticipation that seemed to fuel them all and spur them on. More than half of their traveling days were behind them. Not that their troubles were ended. They all knew better than that.

The land rolled on. The wagon wheels creaked monotonously. The hills lifted into knobs and ridges. Grass became taller and big trees were mixed with scrubby timber. Passing a few makeshift tombstones once in a while did not lift their spirits. No one mentioned them. They just silently grieved for the poor man, woman, or child who did not finish the journey.

THIRTEEN

Mrs. Weston to the Rescue

"*If I didn't have you,* Ann, to keep me company, this trip would be dreadful and pitiful. My feet hurt." Julie brushed a lock of hair from her forehead as they finished filling their water buckets at a nearby stream.

The girls turned to climb up the bank, when Mrs. Weston came over the rise leaning pathetically on her cane with every step.

Julie and Ann offered to fill her bucket for her. When it was filled, they walked with her back toward camp.

"Thank-ee, lassies, this is most kind of ye. You're good girls."

Why, she's rather touching with her funny, toothless smile. I just can't help but like her and pity her at the same time, Ann thought to herself.

Julie gave Ann a knowing glance, and Ann understood she felt the same, strange sympathy for the old woman.

Suddenly a thin, scared voice called out of nowhere. "Annie, Annie, where are you? I can't see you." It was Ozro. Apparently, he'd followed the girls unnoticed and now was lost and confused in the tall grass. Ann could tell he wasn't far away, but she didn't know how to direct

Mrs. Weston to the Rescue

him. She looked helplessly at Julie and Mrs. Weston.

Mrs. Weston stopped. "Tell him to look up and watch for my hat."

She took off her black, tattered, man's hat, put it on her cane, and poked the cane straight up in the air.

"Look up, Ozro, and slowly turn around. Do you see a hat in the air?" Ann called.

"I see it! I see it!" he yelled back. "I'm coming!" Then out from the tall grass young Ozro appeared. He ran straight for Ann, but stopped short when he saw Mrs. Weston and her hat. He hadn't been that far away. He had just panicked.

"Now then, young-un, that's a clever 'nuf trick, ain't it?" Mrs. Weston asked. "Me own mither had to find me one day a long time ago by doing just that."

Ozro nodded his head hesitantly and held on to Ann's hand. They ambled along together, the three children walking slowly, keeping pace with Mrs. Weston.

"Hear that red bird?" Mrs. Weston pointed at the bird who was chirping loudly at them as they walked along.

"He's showin' off his beautiful feather coat and wants us to take note of him, don't ya think?" She winked at Ozro, her wrinkled face brightening with a smile.

The woman seemed to enjoy talking.

"See that big, white cloud up yonder? Now don't that look jest like a willa' tree?"

She chattered on, pointing to birds and trees and to little green plants, herbs, and flowers growing along the ground.

Ann: 1833-1897

"You know lots of things about nature and wild things, don't ya' Mrs. Weston?" Julie commented.

"Waalll, I s'pose I do," she drawled. "But, horse feathers, you can learn and know the same things I know, if you keep your eyes and ears open to what's goin' on about ya. It's a big world out there and lots to be seen and enjoyed."

The children walked Mrs. Weston back to her wagon, then returned to their own. The girls admitted she was a nice but misunderstood old lady, and they agreed they felt sorry for her.

When Ozro excitedly told his folks about the meeting with Mrs. Weston and how she found him, the family was surprised but pleased.

"We never know what goodness is in people until we bother to take time to get acquainted. I see we have somewhat misjudged that woman," Mother observed.

"Now, my boy," said Father, "don't you go walking in the tall grass ever again. I've a mind to give you a sound spanking. You know we warned you of such danger and we told you to stay on the trail. Do you remember?"

Ozro nodded his head sheepishly. "Yes, Papa, I remember. I'm sorry."

The next day the Westons left the wagon train. They had reached their destination. They had not made themselves particularly friendly to anyone, but each family said a polite goodbye.

Both Mother and Father made a point of shaking Mrs. Weston's hand. Now was not the time to nurse hard feelings. "Thank you so much for helping to find my son. I'll

Mrs. Weston to the Rescue

always be grateful to you. May the good Lord go with you," Mother told her kindly.

"'Twas nothing, missus. You have nice young-uns."

Ozro thanked Mrs. Weston, too, and handed her a wild flower he had picked.

Doc Willoughby checked Toby's leg one last time.

"Don't put your weight on that leg for another week. Keep using the cane I gave you."

Toby smiled and shook the doctor's hand. "Thanks, Doc." Then quietly Toby whispered, "Please, Doc Willoughby, tonight give this to Oscar." And he slipped an old arrowhead into the doctor's hand.

"Why don't you give it to him yourself, Toby?" Doc took Toby by the arm and carefully turned him around. There stood Oscar.

"Hey, Oscar, here's somethin' for ya. Mebbe you'll like it." Toby held out the arrowhead. "I found it in some withered grass in an old battlefield back home. Edgar and I thought ya might like havin' it."

"Wow, thanks, Toby. 'Bye and good luck with your leg."

Their fences were mended.

The Westons were off.

FOURTEEN

Rascal

It was just two days later that Ann awoke feeling Dixie's body stiffen in the early morning hours. Her hand had been resting on the dog, and then she heard and felt him grumble ever so slightly. Oscar, too, noticed the dog's nervous reaction, and he turned to squint at Ann. It was just barely light, the sky still had a star or two gleaming dimly.

Father had been sleeping under the wagon with the children, and he now stirred from his sleep. The low voices of the men on duty could be heard off to the side of the wagon train as they talked to Lute and Mr. Hathaway, but there did not seem to be any danger in their voices.

Curious Oscar joined his father in rolling out into the open, Dixie at his side.

"What in tarnation . . . ?" muttered Father as he watched the men approaching with some animal walking between them.

Oscar reached for his father's hand, and Dixie *gruffed*.

Chuckie, too, followed his dad who was also going to investigate the curious happenings. Rubbing his eyes and shaking his head, Chuckie turned to look at Oscar. Oscar was staring straight ahead as he recognized, of all things, the bedraggled Weston dog.

"What's going on?" asked Willard of the men, his puzzled voice low.

"We heard a stirrin' in the grass," whispered Dean, "so we went ta have a look, thinkin' it was a varmint or somethin', and jest look what we found."

Dixie and the other dogs were quietly sniffing the mangy animal but not confronting it.

"Don't this beat all?" asked Orren. "What do we do now?"

The gathering group of men were befuddled, frowning, trying to get their minds up and running—not in anger, but in disbelief.

The Weston dog cautiously made his way over to Oscar and Chuckie, his tail drooping and his head hanging low.

"Why he's gotta be kept," said Oscar, animal lover that he was.

Chuckie gently pulled the dog's head to his side and patted its neck.

"Yeah," Chuckie agreed. "He's no danger to any of us." He looked around at the circle of men. Then turning to his father he said, "Can't our family keep him? Please, Pa. We didn't bring a dog. We could use one."

Dawson was scratching his head. "Who knows where the Westons are by now, there's no way of trying to return the dog. Mebbe they chased him off." He turned to Lute and shrugged his shoulders in a helpless way, not knowing just what to do.

Ann: 1833-1897

"What do ya say, Hathaway?" asked Lute.

Mr. Hathaway was quietly and seriously looking at the poor dog. "I suggest we let the dog fend for himself. We won't chase him away, we'll just wait and see what happens in the next day or two," suggested the wagon master.

"Can't we feed him and help him some right now?" pled Oscar.

"Not unless you want him hangin' around," replied Lute.

"Oh, I'll feed him and help him," volunteered Chuckie immediately. "Please, Pa?" He turned again to his father.

Dawson Dunbar was as stunned as the rest of the men. He rubbed his chin as he struggled to size up the situation. "Do you think he's healthy enough to have around? Let's have Doc Willoughby take a look at him before we make any quick decision, son."

The group nodded and consented that was the wise thing to do.

"Time will tell the wiseness of your decision, Dawson," said Mr. Hathaway, "but I have no objection."

"So you s'pose he deliberately wandered off 'cause he got sick and tired of being treated like a dog?" suggested Dean with a smile.

Oscar caught the wry humor in Harry's words. "They kicked him and never fed him much. Poor thing. They never even gave him a name, just called him 'Dawg.' Made me mad."

"I hardly blame the ole rascal for runnin' off." Orren wagged his head. "He'd had enough! Seems to me he longed for a better life."

Rascal

"I quite agree," said Dawson.

Oscar sensed approval in Mr. Dunbar's voice, and before anyone changed his mind Oscar quickly turned to Chuckie and asked, "What ya gonna name him?"

"Uncle Merton said it right. He's a brave rascal for runnin' off," Chuckie replied. "Guess we'll call him Rascal. Sure suits him."

The men couldn't help but chuckle as they began going back to their wagons.

"Well, it's breakfast time. Let's all have somethin' to eat, includin' Rascal," said Dawson, his eyes sparkling playfully as he looked down at his son and placed his arm around the boy's shoulders.

From her bed under the wagon, Ann had watched the proceedings. Dixie had returned and plopped himself down beside her.

The sun was just now beginning to light the sky with a golden glow.

So the travelers added a new sojourner—a wayfaring dog named Rascal—who soon won the hearts of everyone by turning out to be a gentle, loving dog with a tail that wagged joyously whenever anyone spoke to him, and eyes that made him quite handsome as he cocked his head if someone said his new name.

Rascal, indeed!

The farther west they went, the more Ann took note of the scenery. Little creeks and streams wound between

Ann: 1833-1897

green willows. Someone said they were going toward Lake Michigan. She saw the prairie land flow for miles ahead of her.

Mr. Hathaway said the land rolled like that all the way to the Mississippi River. He also told them that wolves followed their train now, although everyone seemed to know that already. Sometimes a pack of them could be seen off on the horizon, and at night they were outlined against the sky. They would howl in the distance, but Ann would be so tired that the sound didn't bother her.

Then one night Ann wakened to hear Erv's voice. "Come quick, Hannah. Herb's sick."

Mother grabbed her wrap and scurried to follow Erv. They talked softly as they walked. "Let's stop and get Doc Willoughby," Mother recommended urgently.

Please, Lord, Ann prayed when she could no longer hear her mother's footsteps, *let's not have one of those tombstones be a memorial for young Herb or anyone else in our wagon train.*

Ann slept fitfully. Mother did not return until morning. Ann saw her talking soberly to Father. Then she gathered the children around her and explained that Herb was very sick. Doc thought he may have eaten something that didn't agree with him or maybe he'd been poisoned by some berries he'd picked.

It was a sobering time for everyone. Even the sunny day seemed gloomy.

As they walked along, Julie told Ann in a quiet voice, "I had a little brother, Stanley, but he drowned in Deer

Creek when he was only 2. I don't talk or think about it much anymore, but it was awful. I was only 5 at the time, but I can remember it plain as day."

Ann listened intently. There seemed nothing to say to such a sad thing.

"We were on an outing. My grandma had Stanley in a canoe with her at the time, along with two other children. Just what happened, we'll never know, but the canoe tipped over, and in trying to save Stanley, Grandma herself drowned." Her voice dropped even lower. "So did Stanley. Grandma wasn't a strong swimmer, anyway. The other boys could swim and they managed to make it."

"Oh, how dreadful!" Ann's heart went out to Julie. Now she began to see why Chuckie was especially nice to Oscar, perhaps seeing in him his own lost little brother.

"Yes, it was truly dreadful. I was some scared of swimming after that, but I got over it. I like to swim now, and I'm glad.

"Ma took the drowning so hard. She just stayed in bed for a long time. But Pa and Doc and Mrs. Willoughby took care of her. In time she got over it in a way," Julie recalled. "But you never forget, leastways I never have."

Ann could understand how the elderly doctor would be helpful. He was dignified but friendly and always had a twinkle in his eye.

"Chuckie'd like to be a doctor, and Doc says he'll see to it that Chuckie gets to go back to Massachusetts for training when the time comes," Julie added.

Ann: 1833-1897

"Now that we've left New York, I don't think I want to go back east," Ann said, "but I do dreadfully miss my Grandpa." She sighed. "Grandpa often said that he looks forward to the great resurrection morning when we will be reunited with our loved ones. Do you believe in heaven, Julie?"

"Oh, I truly do." She gazed wistfully into the sky. "I want to see little Stanley again and give him a hug. Pa says that when we get to heaven Stanley will be able to swim in the River of Life."

"What will your folks do when we get to Wisconsin territory?" Ann asked her.

"Pa wants to have a little store, and become a tavern keeper and provide for overnight guests. He thinks that maybe he'll set up a post office too. I think it will be fun to help run the store. What do you want to do? Do you have great plans for when you grow up?"

Thoughtfully, Ann remarked, "I think I'd like to be a teacher. I never considered it much, but seeing and watching Elizabeth has given me something to think about. Grandpa and Grandma said every child should know how to read. Mama and Papa help us learn from the Bible, and now I can read anything—books, journals, newspapers, anything I can get my hands on. I'd like to teach children to read."

"I love reading, too," said Julie. "My ma is disgusted when she hears people say that children need to learn how to work and not sit idly and read. They preach real righteouslike and claim, 'Idle hands are the devil's workshop.' Believe me, that really raises Ma's dander, and Pa says, 'Helen's no one to deal with when she's angry!'" Julie's eyes danced with amusement.

"Our old neighbor, Archie Lathrop, thought reading was a waste," Ann laughed. "My ma had told him that children who can't read will be disadvantaged in life. The old fellow slapped his hat on his leg and walked away. But he had the last word," Ann chuckled. "He yelled at my father, 'Willard, your woman's a danger to be around. Kids has gotta grow up fast these days, 'specially if they's gonna git ahead. Why don't ya' make 'em rough, tough, and ready rather than teachin' 'em to read?'"

The girls laughed just thinking about it.

FIFTEEN

Almost Home

In a day or two, Herb had recovered from his mysterious ailment, so everyone sighed in relief. But misfortune was not far away. As they crossed a river one morning, the Grant's wagon started to tip over. Some of the men nearby raced to help out. Dawson Dunbar and Dean Emerson were closest, and they struggled with the wagon. Gene and Rollie rushed to help. The other men all pulled and shoved and shouted orders to each other. It was tricky for some moments, but then they got it back upright. All that seriously happened was that the Grants lost their flour barrel and their bedding got soaked.

When all were safe across the river, Charlotte Russell brought out her peppermint candy to share with everyone. Hugging Irene Grant, Agnes, and Thelma she said, "That was scare enough to send us all into next week," and she looked like she had one of those Irish tears in her eye. But she smiled and hugged Mrs. Grant again.

Those who had gathered around sucked on the delicious candy.

"Thanks, Mrs. Russell," said Oscar who was never far away when there were Mrs. Russell's sweets to be had.

"Thanks, Mrs. Russell," repeated Ozro dutifully.

"You are very welcome, dearie," she said, and hugged Ozro. Then she turned and hugged Oscar, much to his dismay from the look on his face, although he did not pull away from her.

Ann and Julie saw the hug Oscar was getting and turned around so they could have a private laugh. They were too polite to let Mrs. Russell know that they were amused or that Oscar did not appreciate her display of affection.

"Here have another piece." Mrs. Russell handed out more to each of the children.

Oscar walked over to Ann and Julie. "Don't say a thing to me, not a thing." His eyes were laughing and merry.

"Well," Mr. Hathaway said, "see what teamwork can do? That was marvelous, men. I commend you! The almighty God watched over us, and we are safe and sound. Now, let's get ourselves together again and get organized. We'll stop early tonight and rest and relax."

A wild cheer went up, and Ann wondered if they could be heard way back in New York!

The day the wagon train turned northward along the shore of Lake Michigan as they approached Chicago, Ann knew their journey would end soon. Wisconsin Territory was just ahead. The night before, Mr. Hathaway had told them a bit about Chicago. Everyone sat quietly and had listened to him talk.

"Chicago was established as a city in 1833 and its population is now around 4,000."

Ann: 1833-1897

All of a sudden, the wheels in Ann's mind began turning. She didn't hear another word that Mr. Hathaway was saying.

1833! That's the year that the stars fell! Her heart filled with emotion as she embraced the very idea. Chicago was established at the same time as that important year she had heard her parents speak of many times!

I knew this move was significant and eventful! The night the stars fell was in 1833! She liked thinking of the night that her parents had showed her the falling stars even though she had no memory of it herself. She smiled and a pleasant warmness engulfed her very soul. Somehow she felt close to God when she thought of that night. Then she heard Mr. Hathaway's voice continuing. "Ft. Dearborn is the ancestor of Chicago, but it's been six or so years since the military occupied it. By the way, you children will be interested in this.

"Chicago was named by the Indians. Don't know which tribe, but some say the name means 'wild onion' or 'skunk.'"

He paused while both grownups and children laughed.

"I tend to think another theory is correct; that it means strong or great, such as the great Mississippi River."

Mr. Hathaway continued with other details that the grownups had to consider as they approached the end of their journey. Ann looked at Oscar, and he looked at her. Could it be that they really were almost home. She wondered what that home would be like. Ann fell asleep that night in a deep, peaceful slumber. She could almost hear Grandpa's reassuring voice saying, "Tomorrow will take care of itself."

SIXTEEN

The End of the Trail

The day finally came when they reached Wisconsin Territory. This ended the long journey, and Ann suddenly realized that she had become attached to her wagon-train family. Mr. Hathaway, Lute, and Hawkeye would be headed back to New York. The group would now be parting—each family going its separate way—although they would all be "in the same neck of the woods, so to speak," as Doc Willoughby put it. Ann was so grateful that the Eddys and the Dunbars were actually locating not far from each other.

The grownups wished each other God's speed. "We'll be within shoutin' distance from each other!" said Henry Russell with a laugh. "I hope you will look me up and come see me when I get the saw mill up and runnin'."

"Oh, we will," Dean Emerson assured. And everyone nodded and voiced their agreement.

"Don't forget to visit my store and tavern for overnight guests," reminded Dawson Dunbar.

The group gathered around the wagon master and his assistants, each of them thanking the wagon leaders for a safe trip. Even the young people joined in.

Oscar wove his way through the crowd to get closer to

Ann: 1833-1897

Lute. Lute saw him coming and with a wide grin on his face saluted his young friend, then grabbed him up in a bear hug.

Hawkeye raised his hand to get everyone's attention, then stepped to one side of the group. When everyone was watching he did a cartwheel and a back flip with ease and agility.

The applause was loud and the 'hoorays' were even louder.

"You didn't think you were the only one who could do this, did you, Oscar?" he asked and winked. Then he grabbed Oscar's hand and announced, "Ladies and Gentlemen. Meet the new acrobat team! The Jumping Jacks. Let's show 'em, Oscar!"

Then the two of them did some cartwheels and flips. Afterward, Hawkeye lifted Oscar to his shoulders and the folks heehawed and shouted. The look on Oscar's face was one of sheer delight.

Mr. Hathaway congratulated the families on their successful trip and thanked them for their good spirit and their cooperation.

"The trails and trials have been kind to us all, thanks to the good Lord," he said. And they all agreed, "Amen."

They sang a hymn, and Mr. Hathaway gave a moving benediction.

Then out of the blue Pete Edminster stepped forward. Somewhat hesitantly he cleared his throat and said,

The End of the Trail

"Folks, I have something to tell you all. Linnie Maguire and I have decided to get married. I've talked to Orren and asked permission to propose. He has given us his blessing." He pulled Linnie next to him and kissed her cheek. She blushed modestly, but her eyes were filled with pride and delight.

Everyone gasped, then smiled, and then turned to each other and smiled some more. They had all been expecting this to happen, but it was a pleasant surprise and a nice way to end the journey.

Lute let out a holler and shouted, "Hooray for the bride and groom!"

Folks gathered around Pete and Linnie to hear more of their plans.

"Well," explained Pete, "the wedding won't be until next summer. I have to get settled, and Linnie has to get things ready." He grinned down at his promised bride. Rachel Maguire unabashedly went over to Pete, stood on her tiptoes, and kissed him.

"Did you ever!" said Oscar to Ann and Julie. "I'd be so embarrassed if I were Pete. At least Mrs. Russell doesn't kiss me." He looked down at the grass and grinned from ear to ear.

"Oh, you'll understand when you get older, Oscar," laughed Julie.

"Never, never, no, not ever," he vowed.

When the cheering died down, Orren Maguire shook hands with Pete and everyone shook hands with everyone else. The women hugged each other and sure enough,

Ann: 1833-1897

Mrs. Russell got out her little hankie,

Gene and Rollie hoisted Pete to their shoulders, and Rollie called out, "Everyone better come to the wedding. We're going to have the best and biggest and loudest shivaree that there ever was for the lucky couple. Pete won't get off scot free, not with Linnie's brothers around to help make the commotion. He won't even know what hit him when our celebration starts."

How the crowd roared with laughter.

"We knew it, we knew it, didn't we, Ann," exclaimed Julie. "We knew it all along." And the girls congratulated themselves.

Before they parted, Helen Dunbar and her sister Dorothy Emerson offered to make the wedding gown for Linnie.

It was a glorious ending to a long, long trek into the unknown that had turned out to be happy and successful.

The Eddys and Dunbars followed a stage route trail that was originally marked out by someone dragging a log through the tall prairie grass. This road, of sorts, led them to their new homes.

When their routes parted, the families stopped to say farewell again.

Ann and Julie hugged each other. Julie truly had been the friend Ann had prayed for.

"I'm so glad to have met you, Ann," said Julie. "Without ya this trip would not uv been as much fun.

The End of the Trail

Let's try to visit once in a while."

"We'll soon learn our way around. It won't be long before we get together again," Ann replied. And when Ann reminded Julie that she had been an answer to prayer, Julie's pretty green eyes shone brightly.

They hugged again and said their goodbyes.

Immediately, Mother and Father began to farm a wild, unimproved tract of land that was almost in primitive condition. With the help of the children, they established their home in Wheatland, Kenosha County, in southern Wisconsin.

Indians were still numerous in the neighborhood, and there were many timber wolves and deer. Ann rather enjoyed hearing the mournful howls of the wolves, but she knew she must always be alert and never go out alone at night.

Before winter, they moved into a small log house which they'd built with the help of neighbors. It was cozy and safe. The first night in their new home Ann crawled into her bed in the loft. Then looking through a little window at the starry sky, she prayed, *"I thank Thee, Father, for such a wonderful, safe trip. We were guided, just as the stars of heaven in their orbits are guided by Thee. We were protected and blessed by Thy hand. No lives were lost. We're all safe.*

"When Thou dost come again, please take me home to heaven so I may dwell with Thee forever. And if it be Thy will, Lord, may Julie be my neighbor? I'd be so grateful. Thy will be done.

"Help me to serve Thee for the rest of my life. Amen.

The Rest of Ann's Story

Ann adapted the ways of doing things in her new Wisconsin home. Life depended upon it. It was not as easy to do chores as it had been back in Erie County, but she shouldered responsibility without complaining. And she learned shortcuts and quicker ways of doings things that made her work easier. The wit and wisdom of the saying "There's more than one way to skin a cat," made a whole lot of sense to her now!

The Eddy family became acquainted with another family from western New York who lived not far away. Charles and Mary Ann Turner had come to the new world from Ireland in 1828 with their two older boys, Alexander and William. LeRoy, John, Charles, and Stephen were born in New York, and so was little Martha Ann, who joined the family just before their move to Wisconsin in 1841.

Both the Eddys and Turners bravely persevered and struggled to make a go of their pioneer homes. The Turner boys were hard workers. Oscar enjoyed hearing LeRoy tell how in his early teens he'd helped drive the horses that pulled barges on the Erie Canal. The family shared a love of horses.

The Rest of Ann's Story

Then in May, 1847, Ann's father died. It was only four years after the family began homesteading in Wheatland, Wisconsin. His death was not only a shock and a grief to his family, but left them without a strong man's help in working the farm. The Turner family immediately offered assistance and comfort. John, a strong and sturdy boy of 15, spent every day with Ann's family, helping them with their labors, lifting their loads. Hannah didn't know what they would have done without him. Oscar and Ozro were growing by leaps and bounds and were getting stronger every day, but John knew how to do things the frontier way. Ann and her brothers admired him. He was a steady young fellow—someone they looked up to.

Ann married John on a beautiful fall day, September 23, 1849, in Salem, Racine County, Wisconsin. She was 16 and he 17. What a happy day that was—a simple country ceremony performed by Pastor Burnham. John's brothers and Ann's brothers all helped to make the occasion a happy one!

The young couple continued to help Hannah on her farm, and gradually things went smoother, each one taking responsibility and working with vigor.

Then on April 24, 1851, Ann gave birth to a baby girl. Her parents named her Marilla, after Mrs. Marilla Rogers who was a highly-regarded schoolteacher in a little town not far from Ann's home in Boston, Erie County, New York. The town of Marilla was named for this same teacher. Both John and Ann thought the name was poetic and musical, becoming of their first-born lovely

Ann: 1833-1897

daughter. And so she became—Marilla Arabella Turner.

It was her mother's dream that one of this little girl's life goals would be to get a good education. Ann and John vowed to provide this baby with every opportunity to attend school.

When John's brother LeRoy decided to move north to the New London area, Ann and John went with him. They made their home in the town of Liberty where Marilla attended school and graduated from the eighth grade—something unique and special for a girl of her generation. She more than fulfilled her parents' hopes and dreams.

More About Ann's World

The Night the Stars Fell

Ann was only a baby on November 13, 1833, when her father bundled her up and took her outside so she could see the sky filled with shooting stars. Thousands of people along the Eastern part of the United States and Canada saw them too. Many were afraid, and thought it was the end of the world. But Ann's parents were thrilled, and wanted baby Ann to be with them if Jesus truly was coming that night.

Of course, Jesus did not come on that cold night, but many people thought this was a sign that He was coming soon. Several years later some of the people who happily looked for Jesus' coming started the Seventh-day Adventist church. The word "Adventist" shows that this church looks forward to seeing Jesus come very soon.

Ann's Father Was a Blacksmith

The blacksmith shop was an important part of most towns in the early 1800s. Everyone knows that they made horseshoes, but that was just the beginning. The blacksmith also made door hinges, farm tools, and even utensils used in the kitchen.

Ann: 1833-1897

Heating iron until it could be bent, then shaping it into horseshoes and tools was hot, muscle-building work. It's not surprising that Ann's father had the courage to travel to a new land where they'd start over, building almost everything they needed with the tools they brought with them.

Grandpa Says Goodbye

It's hard for us to imagine a world without cars and telephones, but that was Ann's world. And when Ann's family left Grandpa, he knew he probably would never see them or even talk to them again.

How sad he must have felt to watch them go. How he must have missed Ann and her brothers. But before they left he gave them what he could—small gifts, and his reminder of one of his favorite psalms, Psalm 91. This is a psalm of God's protection and care. Grandpa knew that Ann and her family would need God's care on their long trip and after they got to their new home in the Wisconsin Territory.

Sewing for the Trip

Preparing for the long trip, Mother did all her sewing by hand. That was the only way. Several men in different countries had tried to invent a sewing machine, but there wasn't one for home use. Then in 1844 a young farmer, Elias Howe, invented a sewing machine that worked. Issac Singer was right on his heels with *his* sewing machine. It wasn't until 1889, however, that sewing machines were made to be used in the home.

Did you know that people didn't want sewing machines? It's true. In France, a mob almost killed its French inventor. And in 1834 an inventor named Walter Hunt gave up the idea and invented the safety pin instead! Why didn't people want a mechanical sewing machine? They said that all the people who worked in factories hand-stitching clothing would be put out of work!

"Wagon Ho!"

The trip from New York to Wisconsin Territory was more than 500 miles long.

On today's highways a trip of 60 miles takes an hour or less. But wagons traveled only two miles an hour, not 60!

That gave Ann and the other kids plenty of time to enjoy the scenery—close up. There wasn't room in the wagons for the families to ride, so they walked.

Perhaps Ann's wagon train traveled eight or ten miles the first day. You can imagine how tired she was by the time they stopped. Until their legs grew stronger Ann and her brothers must have taken turns riding up on the wagon seat next to Father who was driving the team that pulled their wagon. Mother probably rode up there too. The problem was that the way was bumpy. Often it was easier to walk than to ride.

Walking... walking... walking

The children on the wagon train must have invented games to play as they walked alongside the wagons. And

Ann: 1833-1897

even though Ann thought sunbonnets were hot and uncomfortable, she would have been glad for the ones her mother had made for her to wear. Under the scorching sun they gave a little shade to her face.

The girls' long skirts surely caught on the weeds, collecting stickers and seed pods and even insects. And there were no rest areas with running water and paper towels along the route either.

Going west with a wagon train was an adventure that continued for several weeks.

Meanwhile Back in the East...

It was about 1843 when the Eddy family made the long trip from their home near Buffalo, New York to the Wisconsin Territory. Unknown to them, in towns fairly close to where they'd lived there was quite an interest in the soon-coming of Jesus. William Miller was using Bible prophecy to explain his belief that soon the world would end, for Jesus was coming. People looked back to the falling of the stars as one of the signs that Jesus was coming soon.

Many years later Ann would learn of Seventh-day Adventists, and that would change her life.